KALEIDOSCOPE DESIGNS

Adult Coloring Book

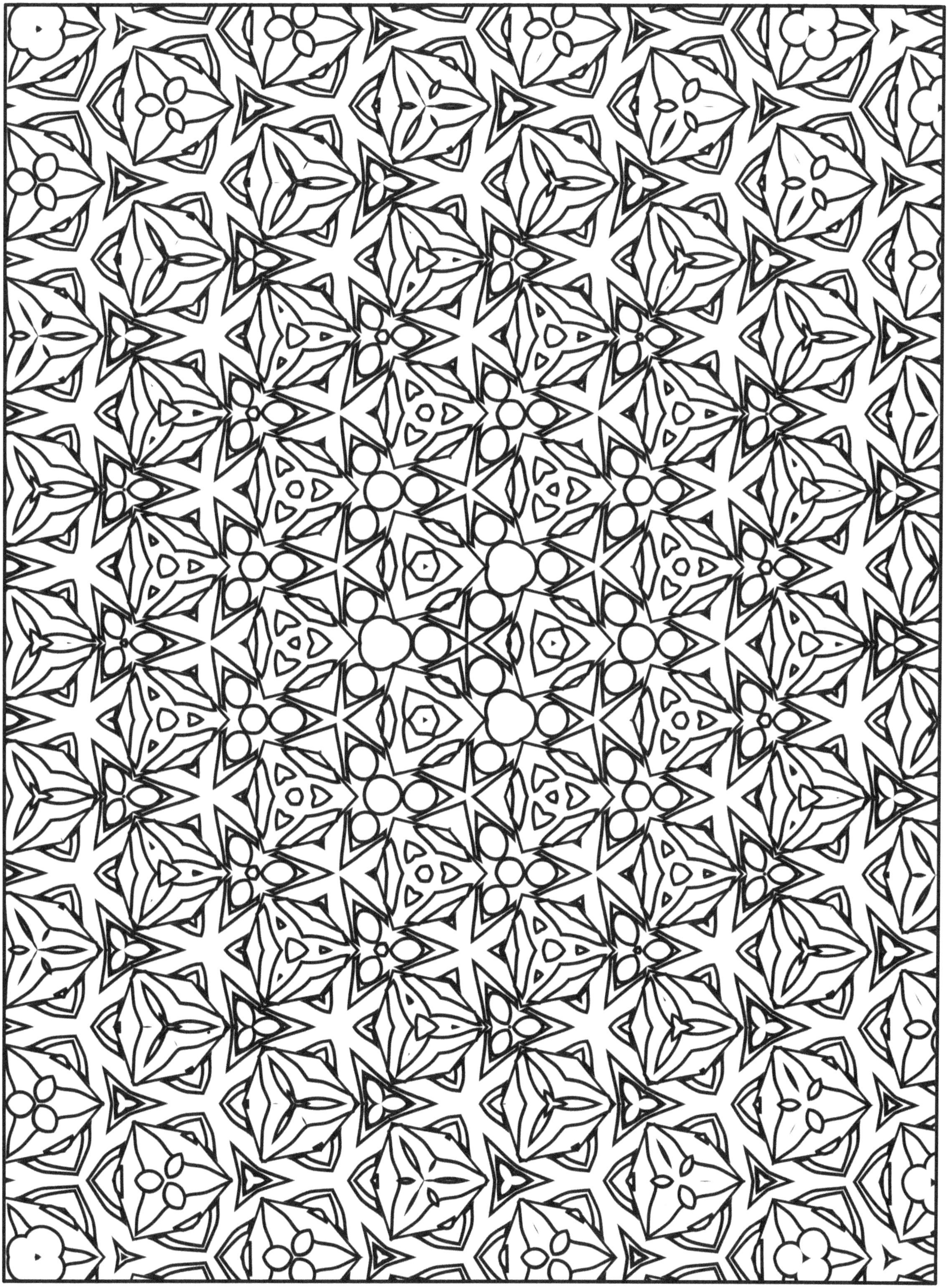

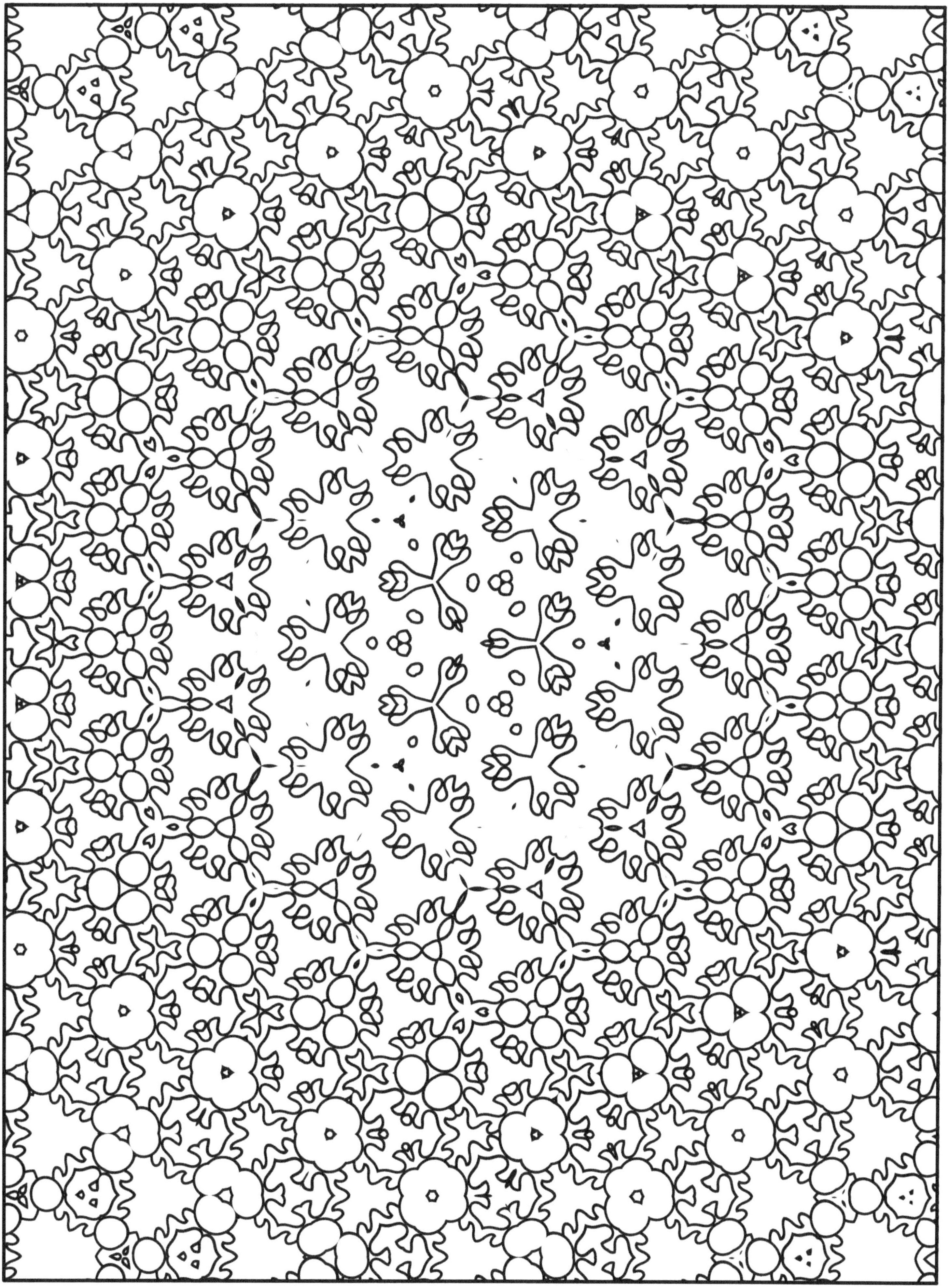

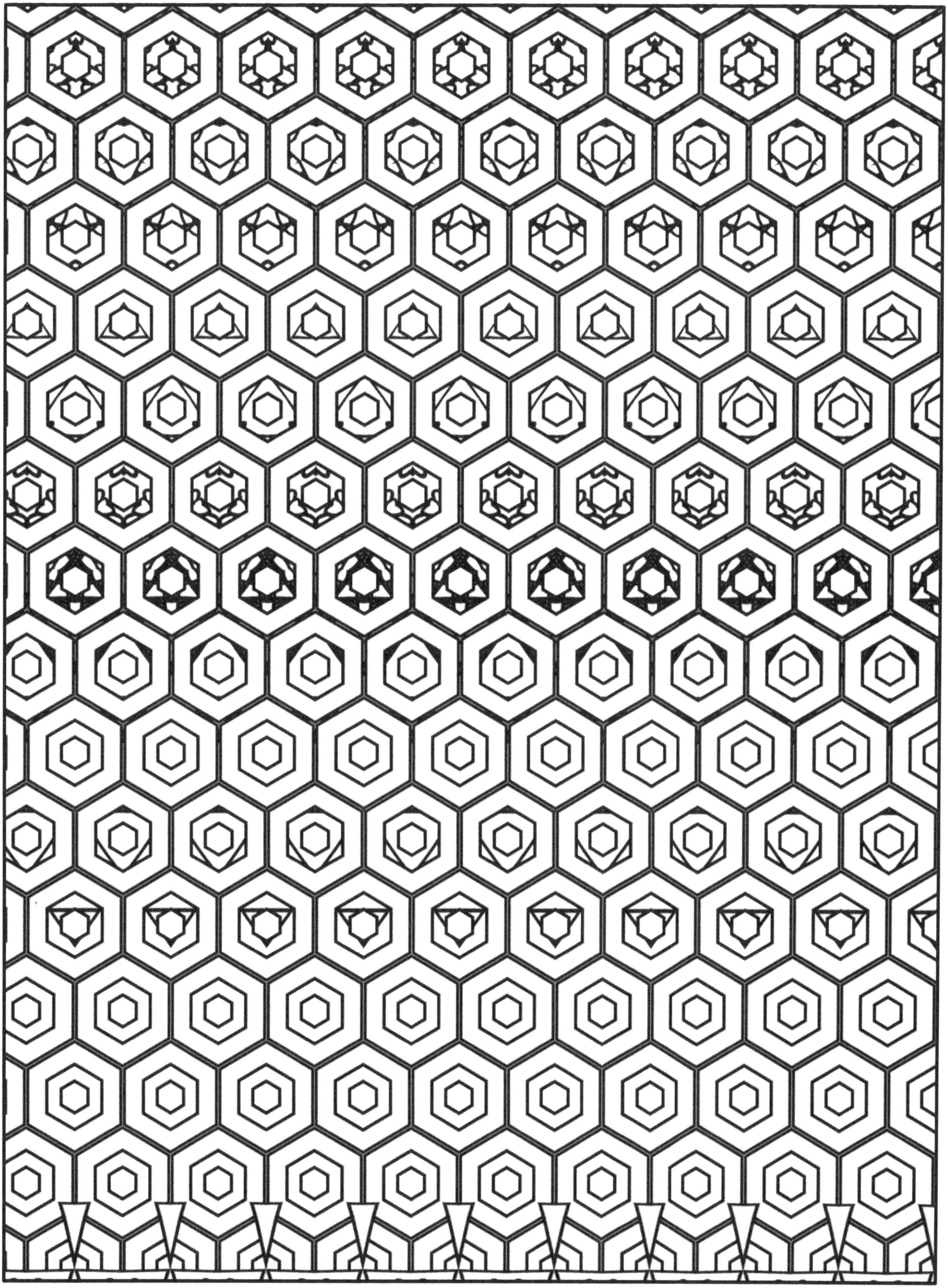

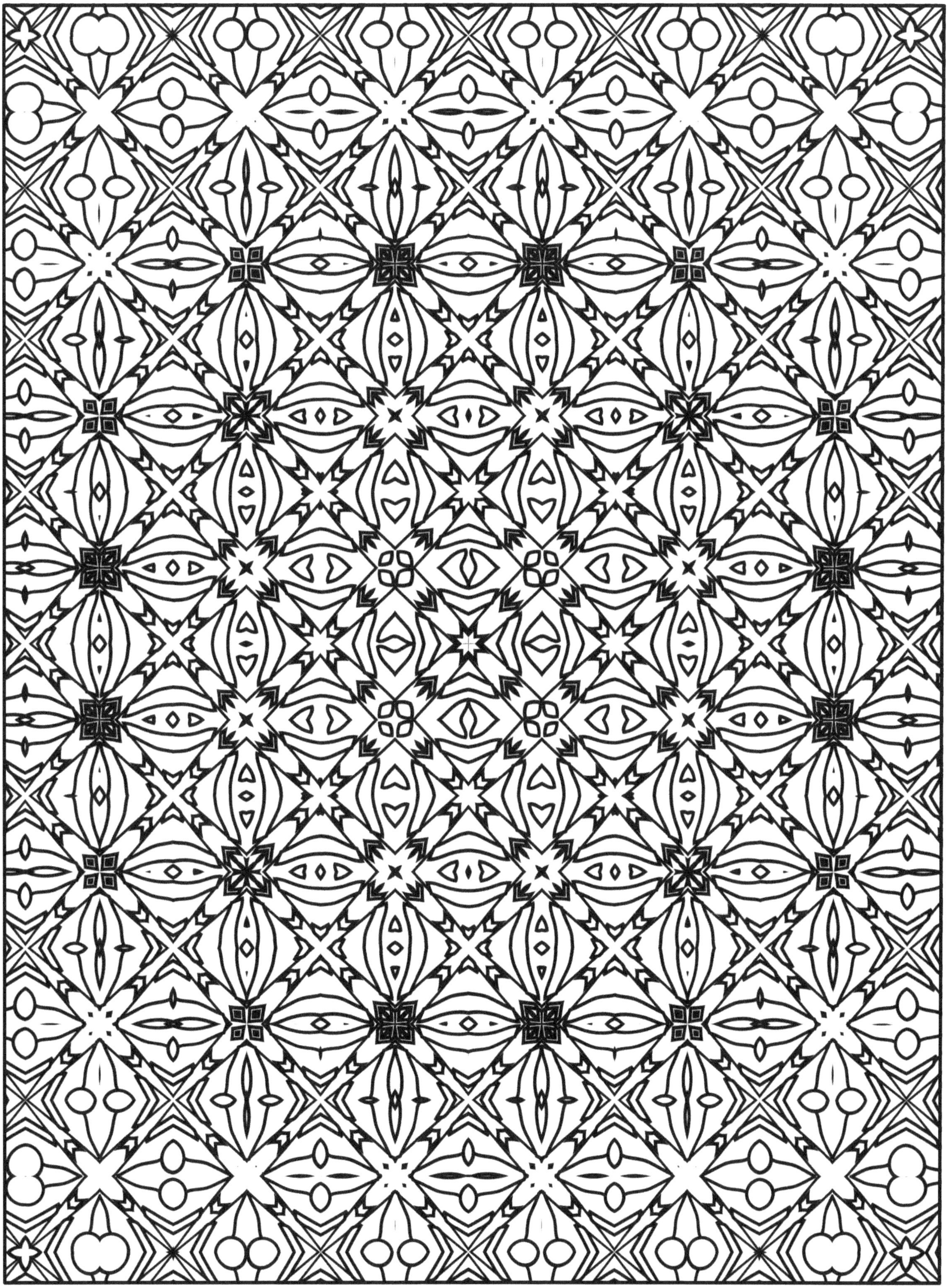

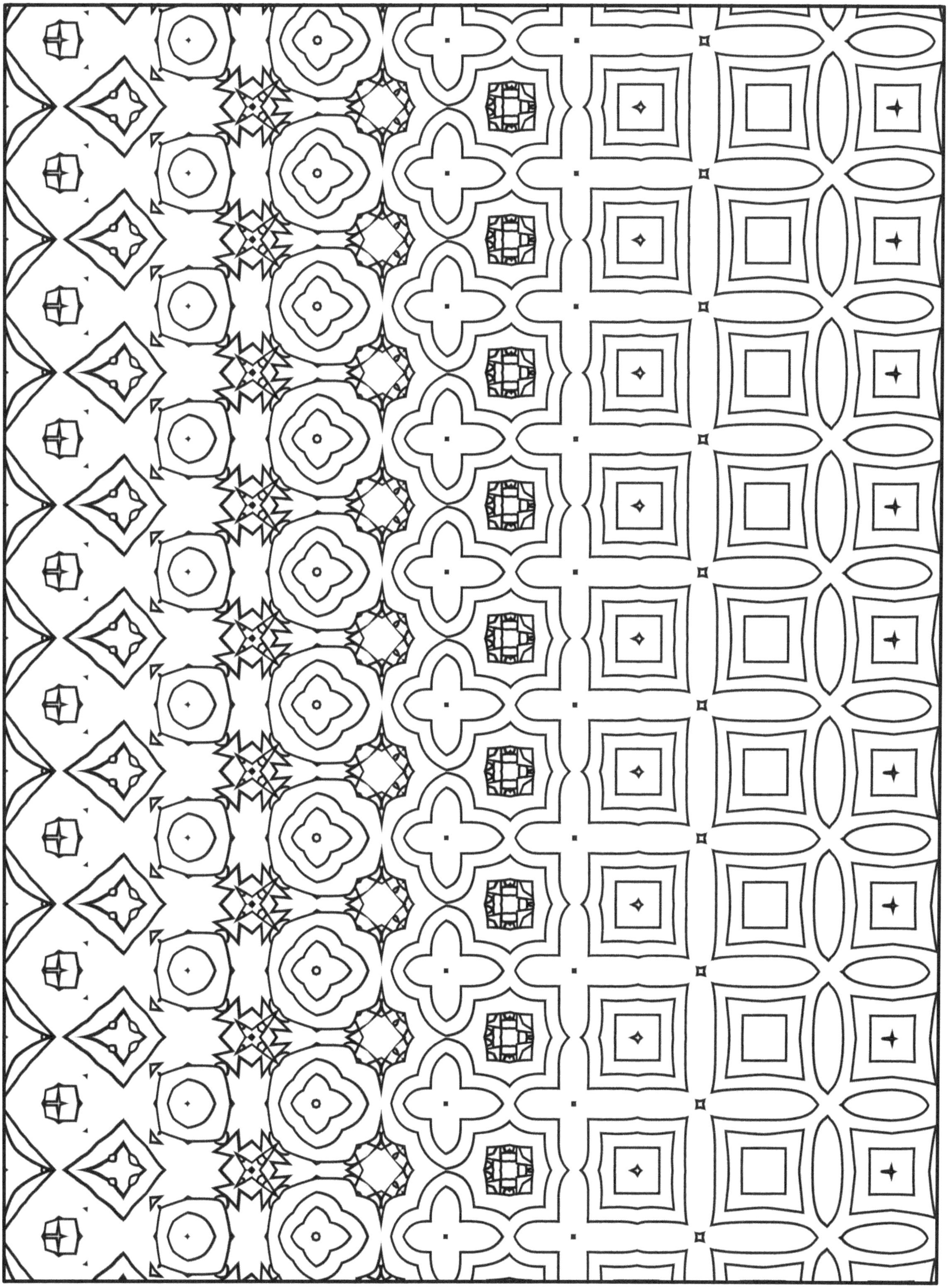

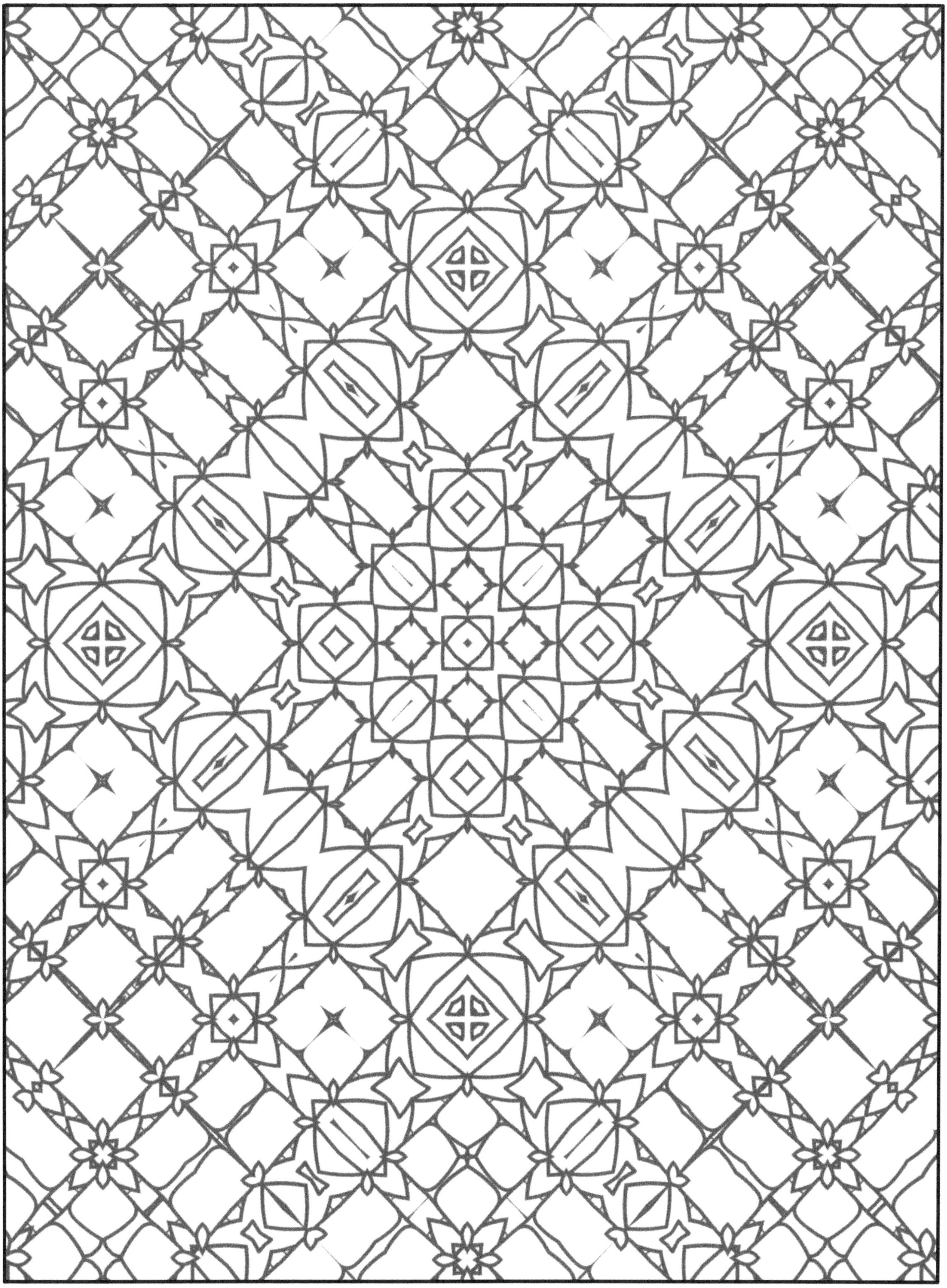

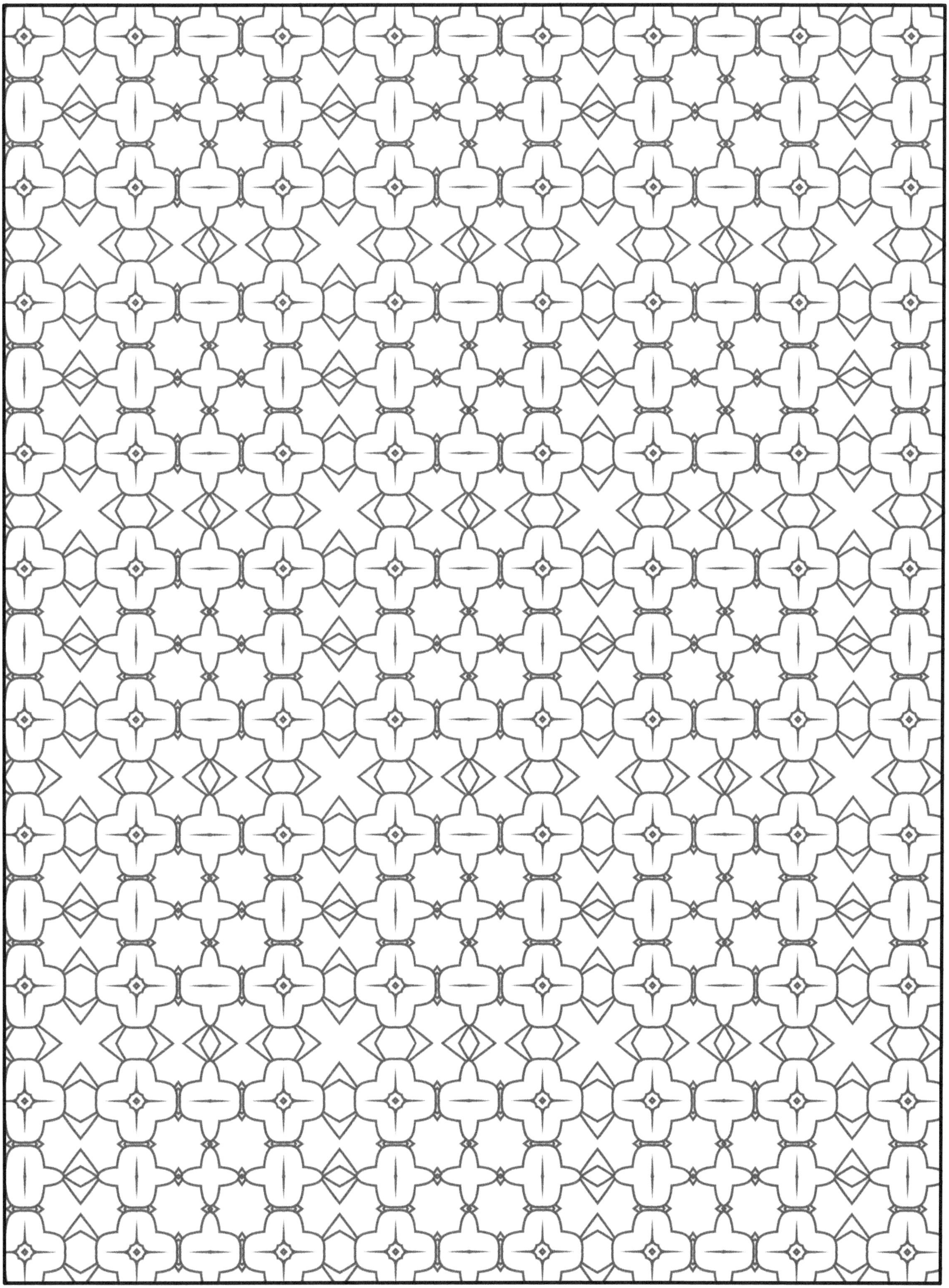

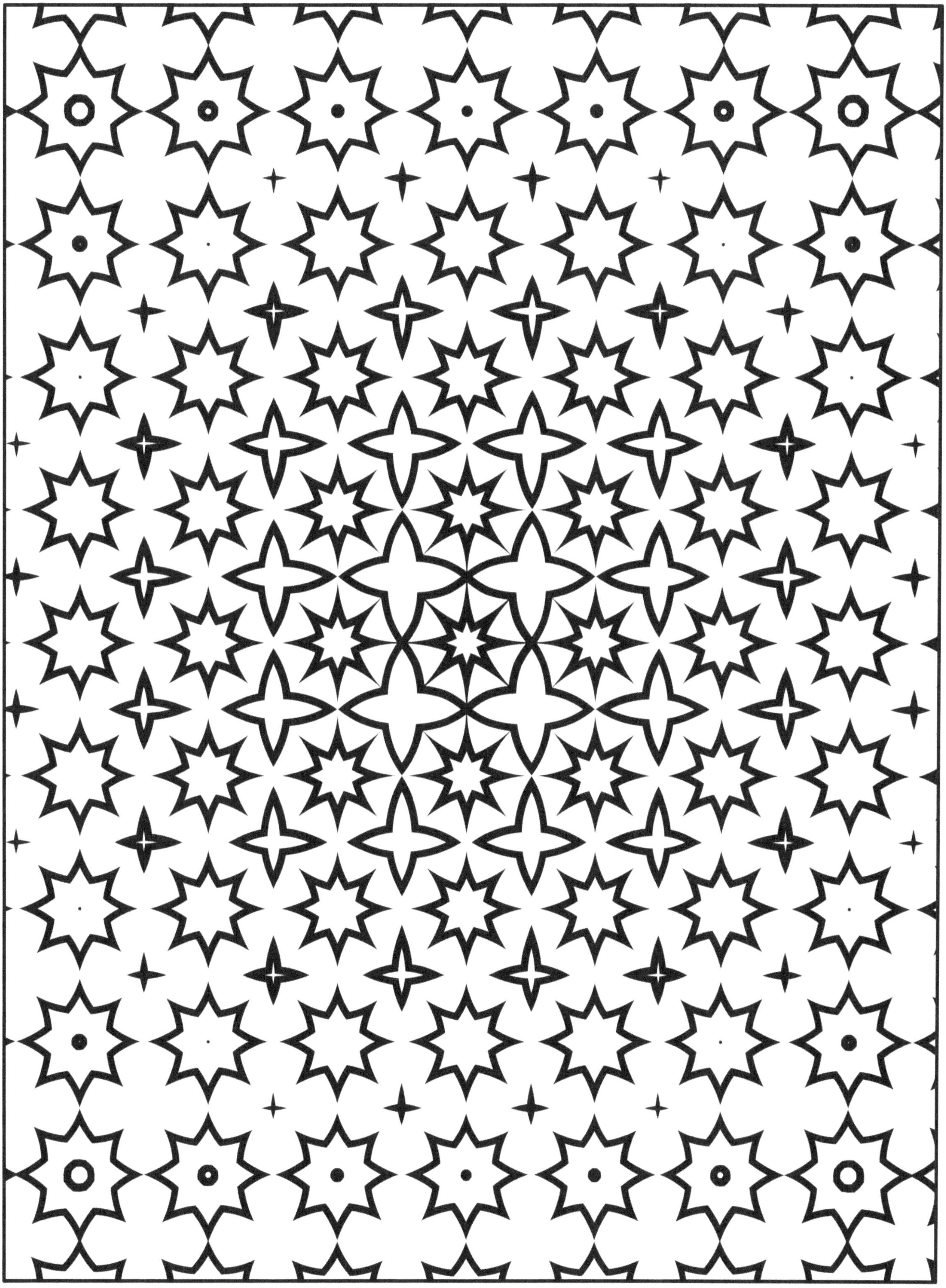

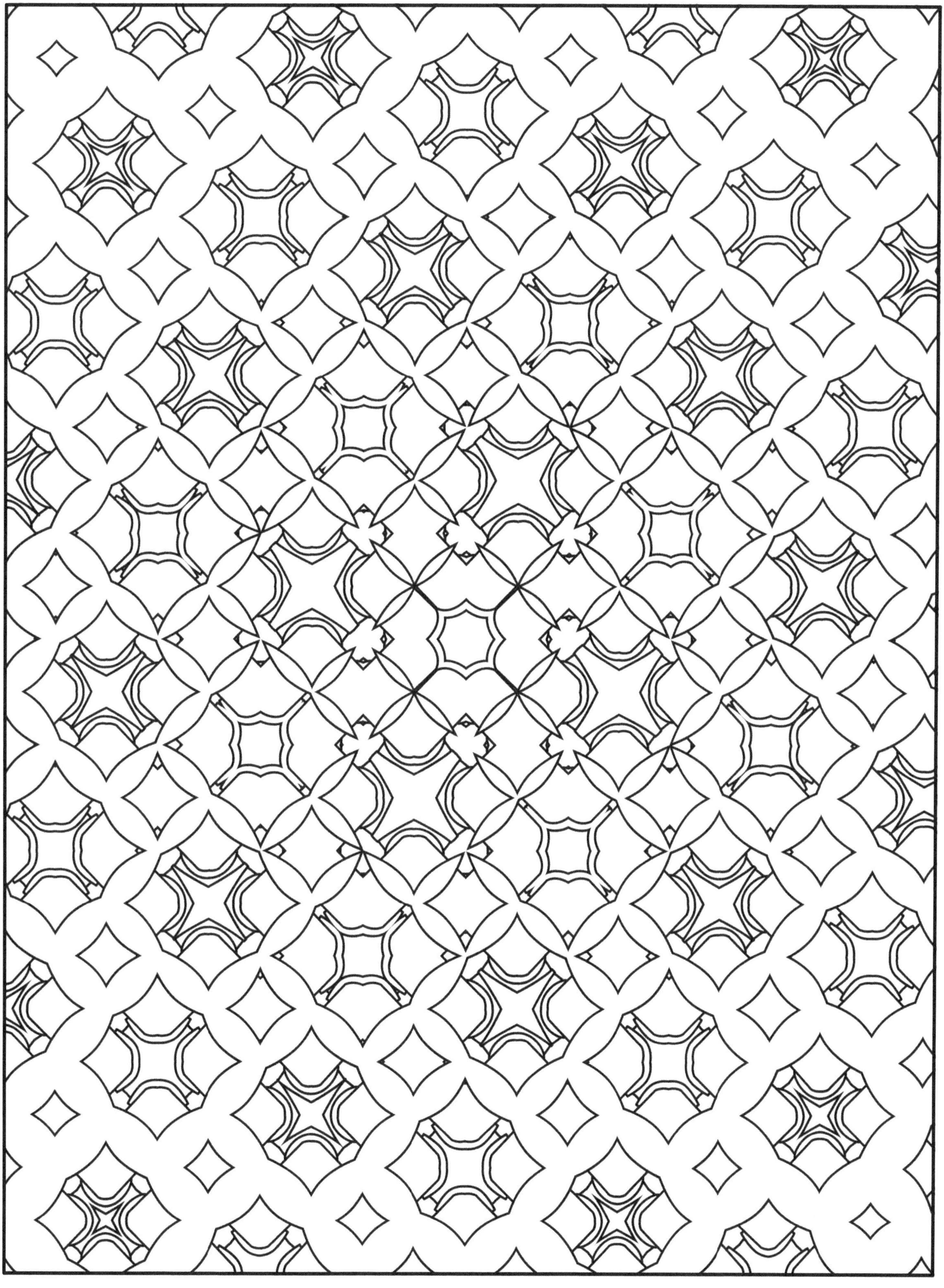

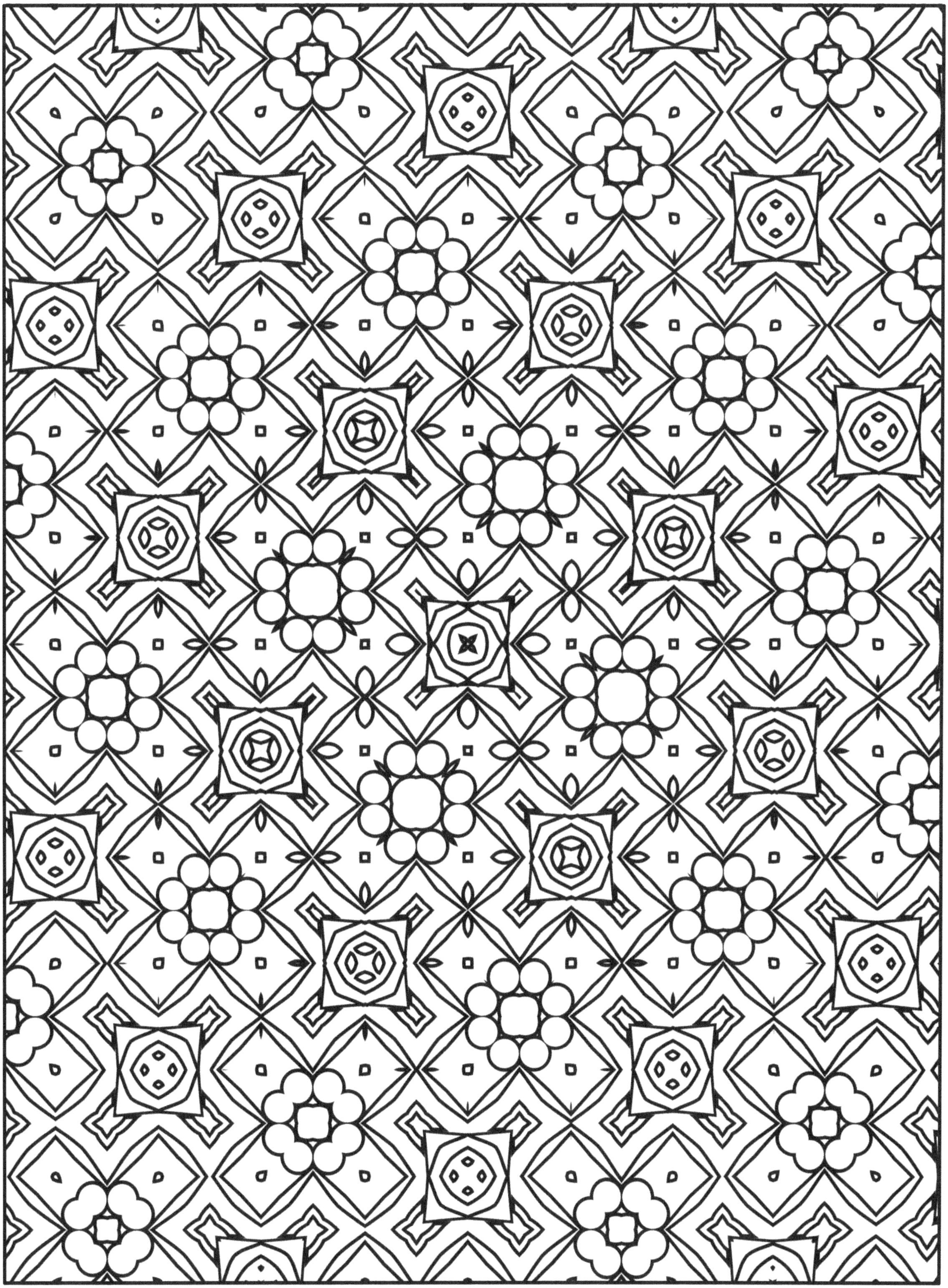

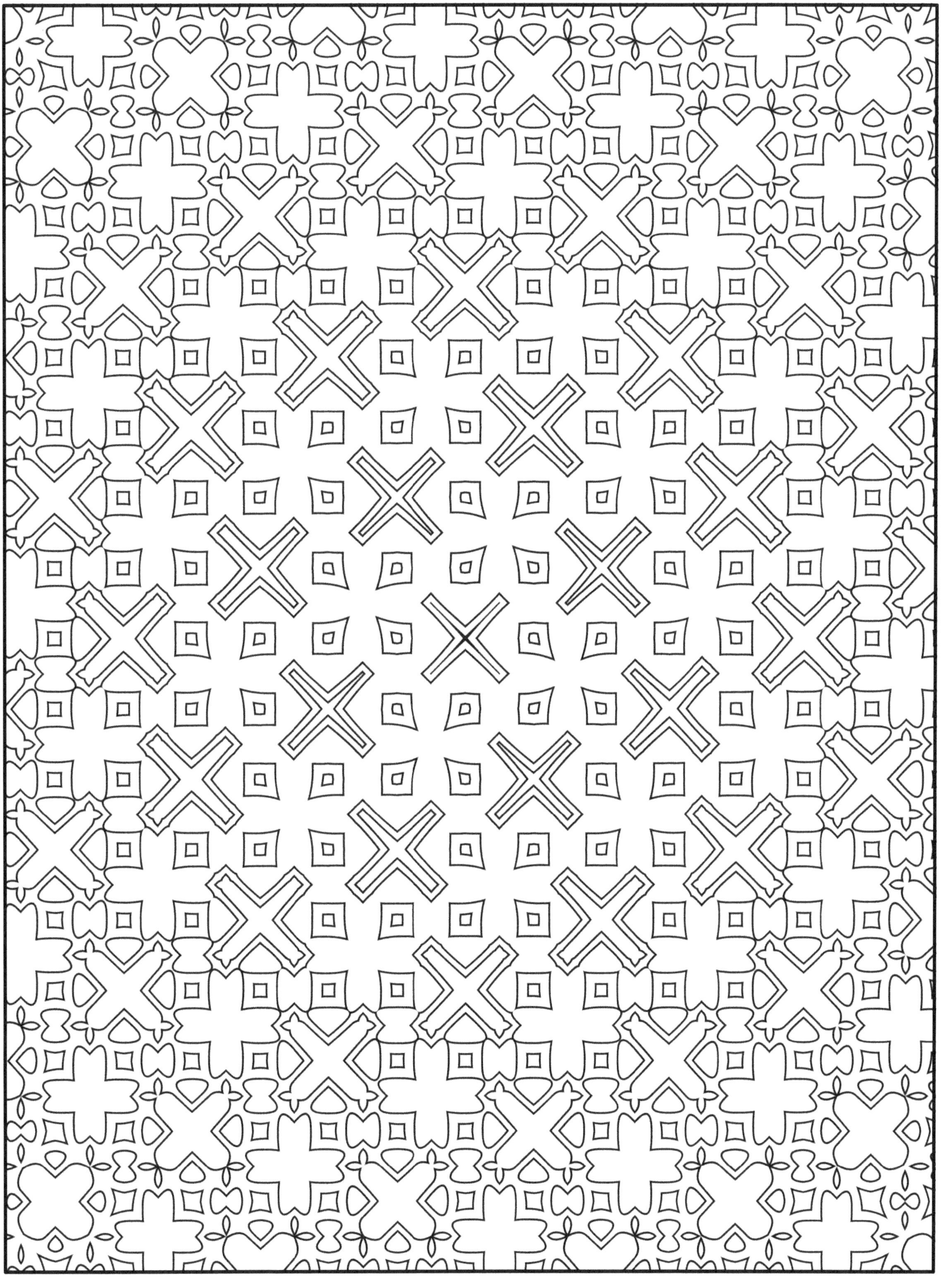

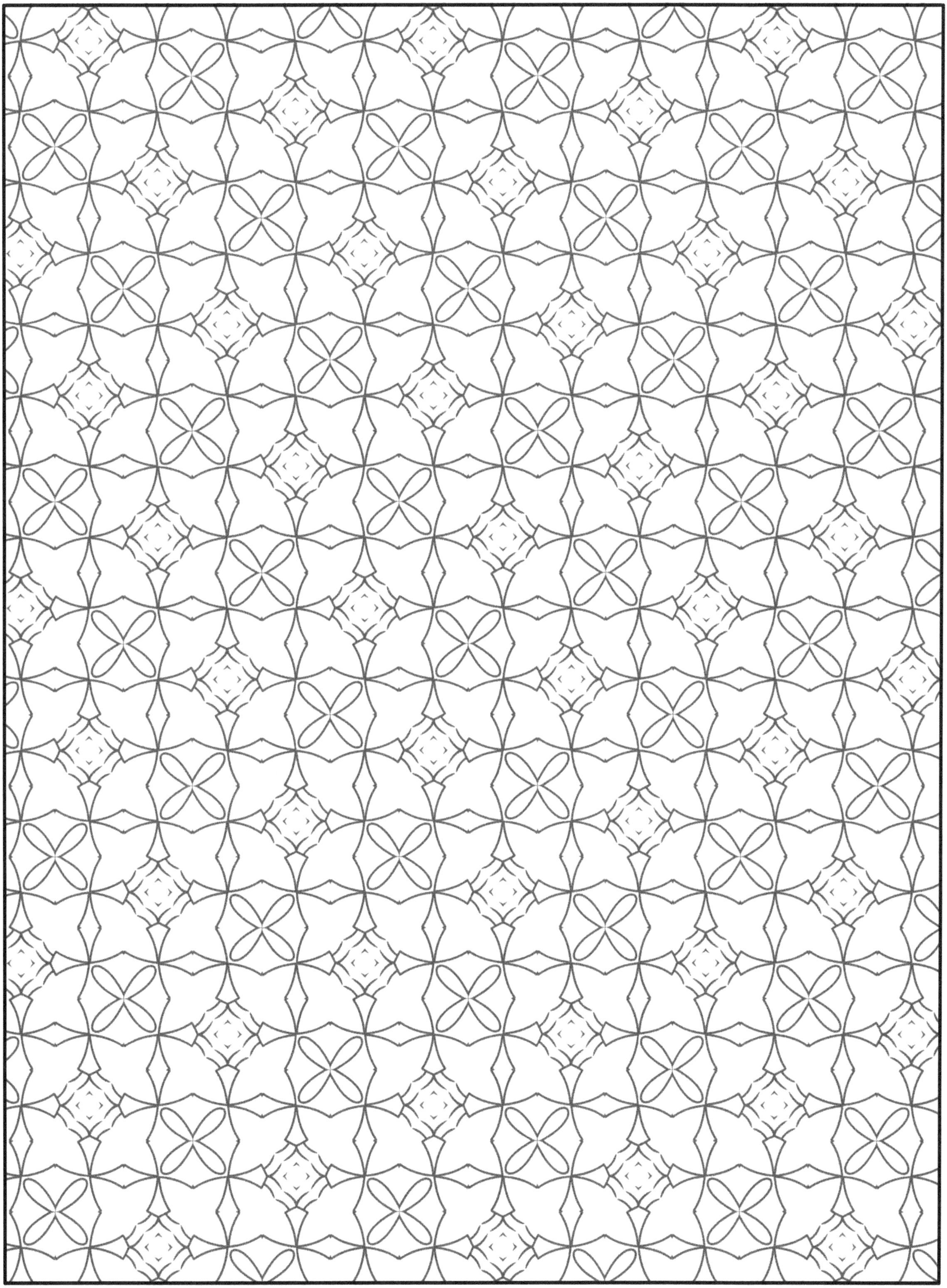

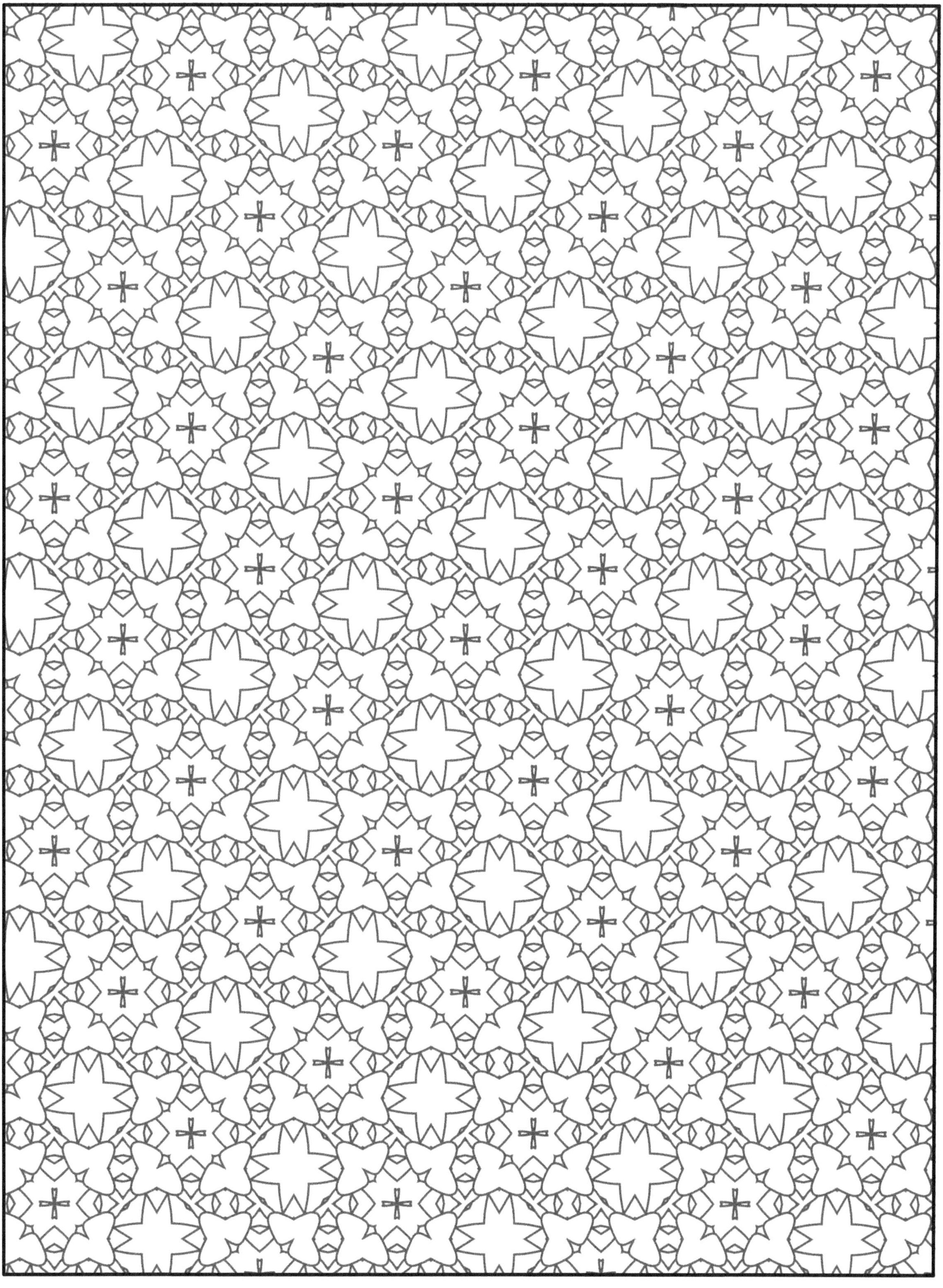

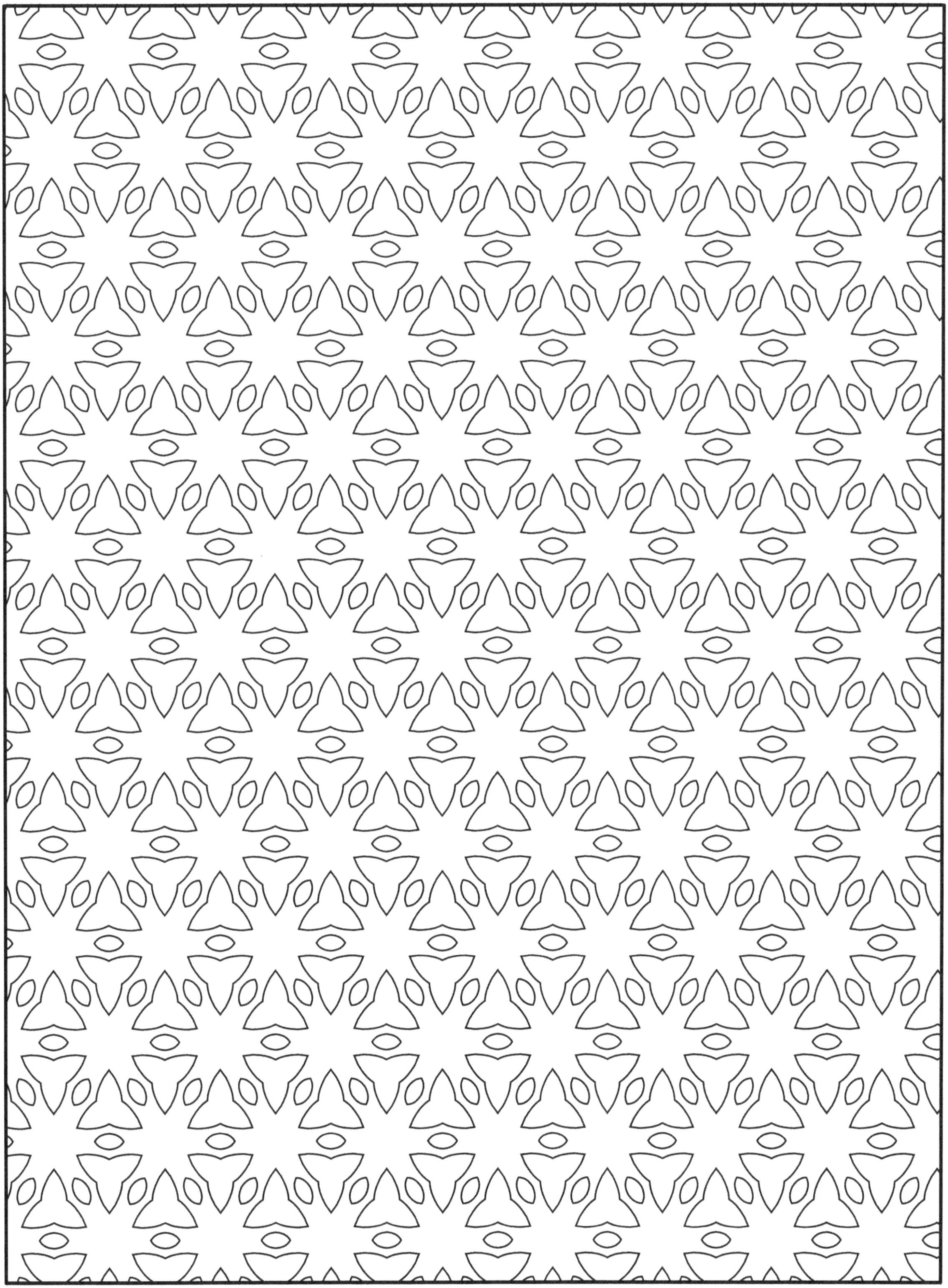

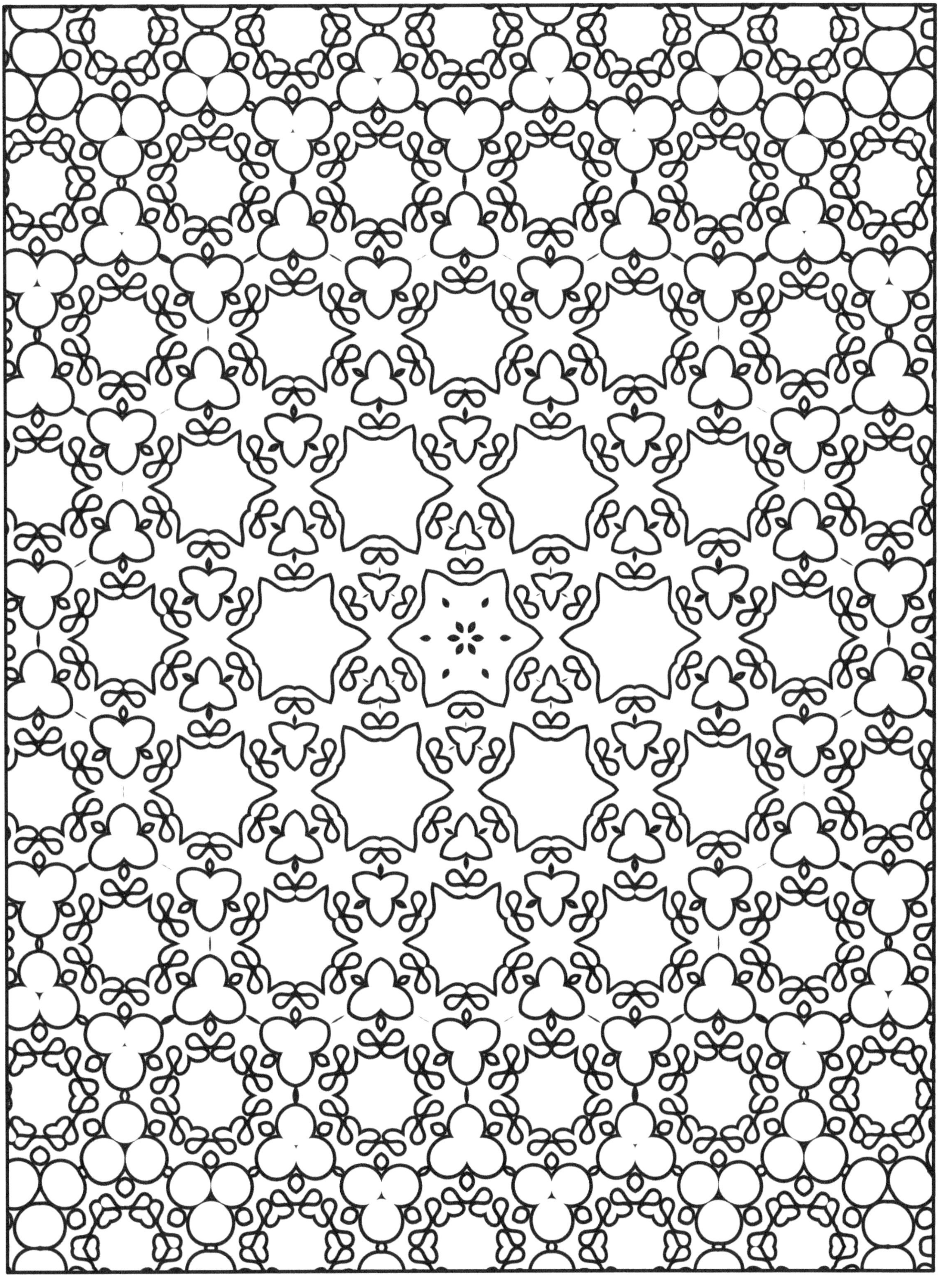

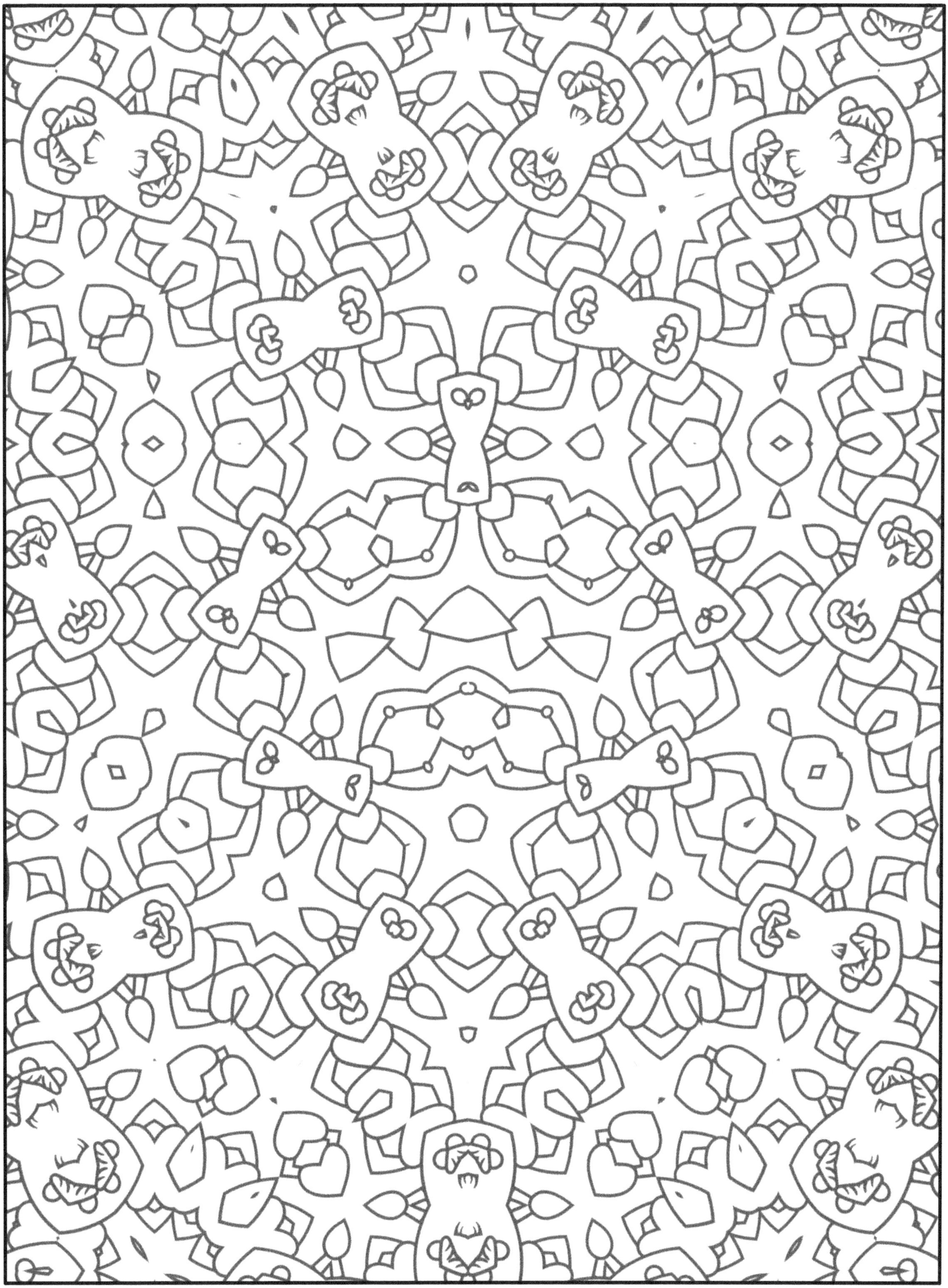

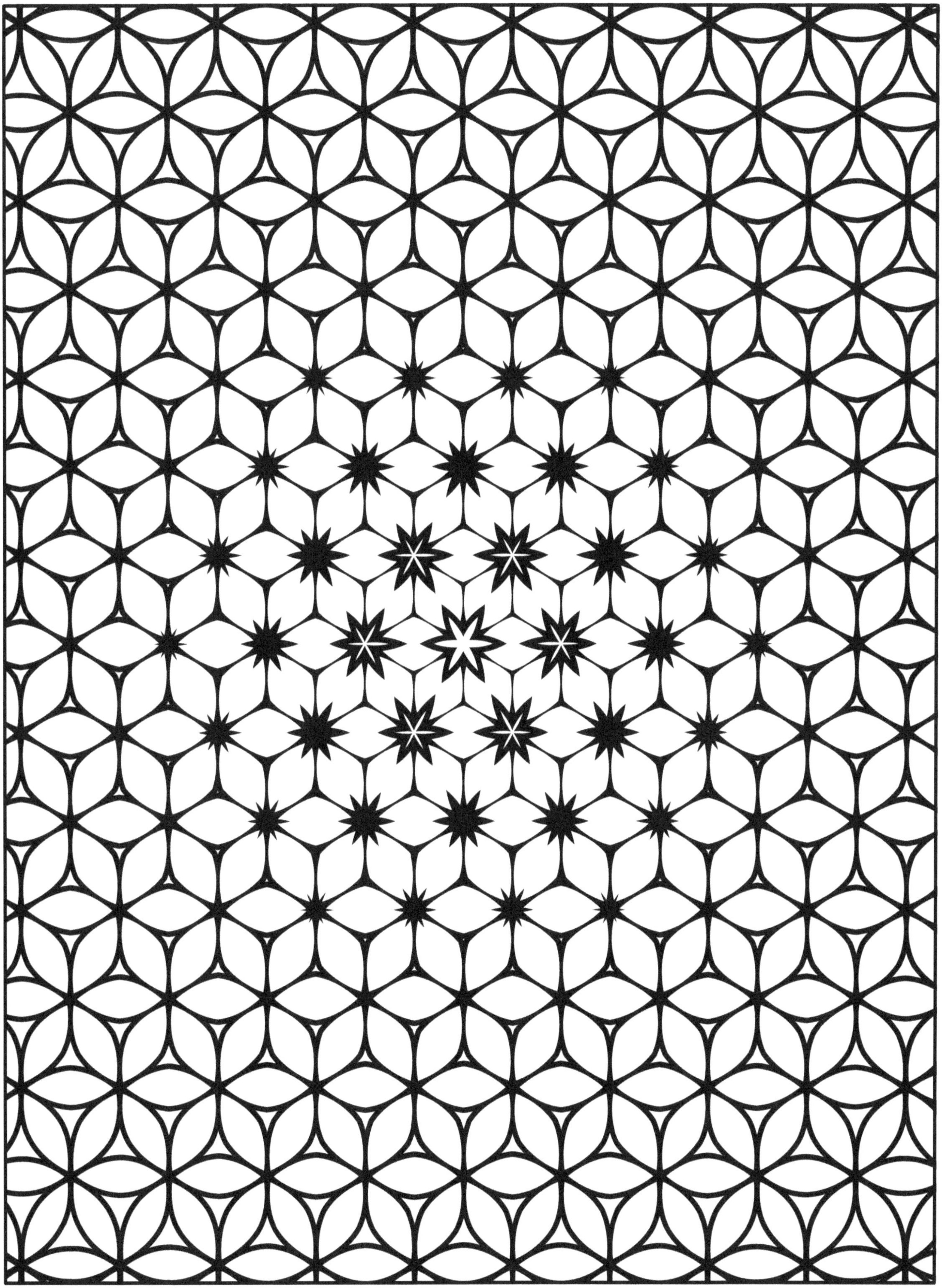

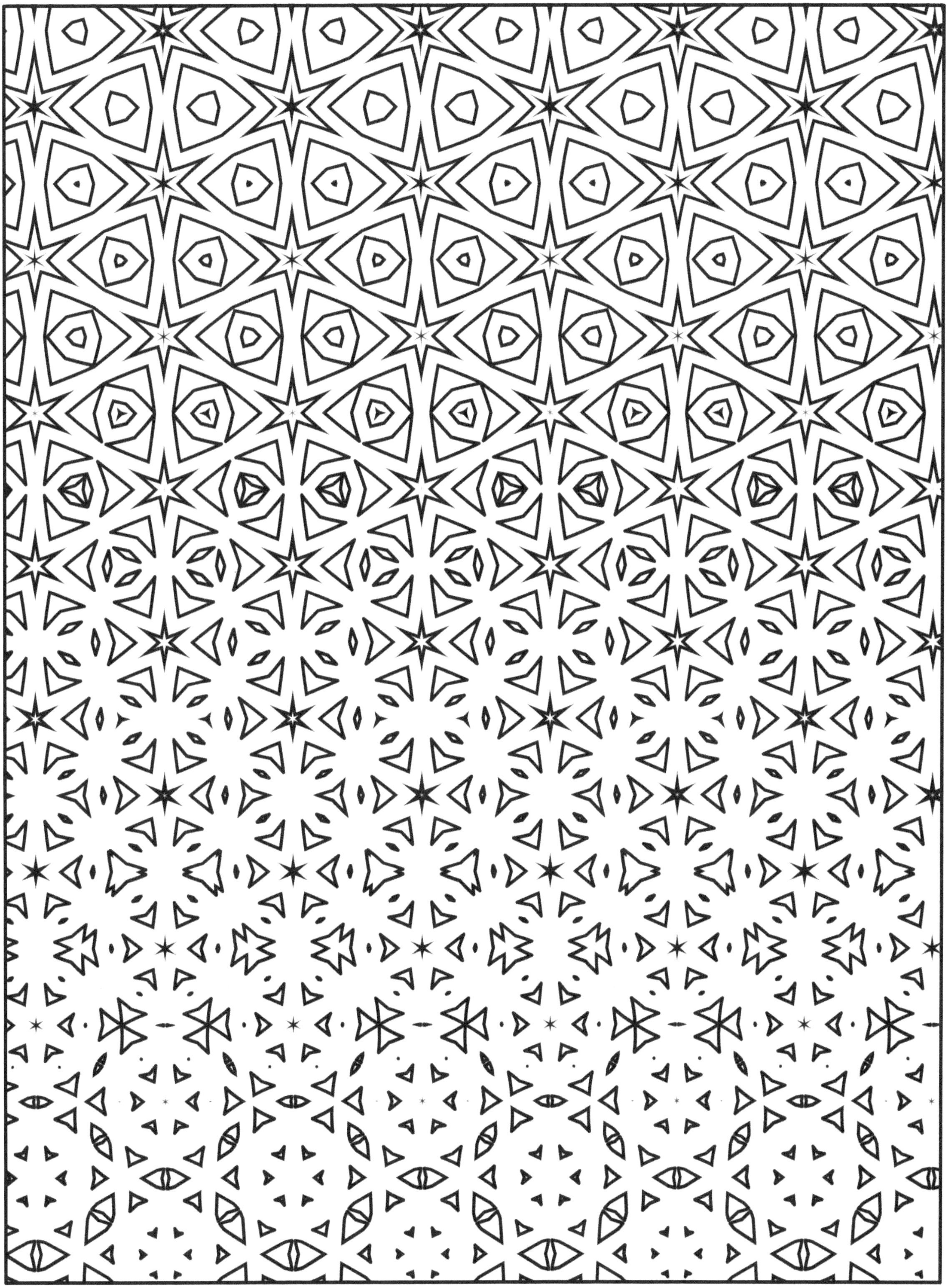

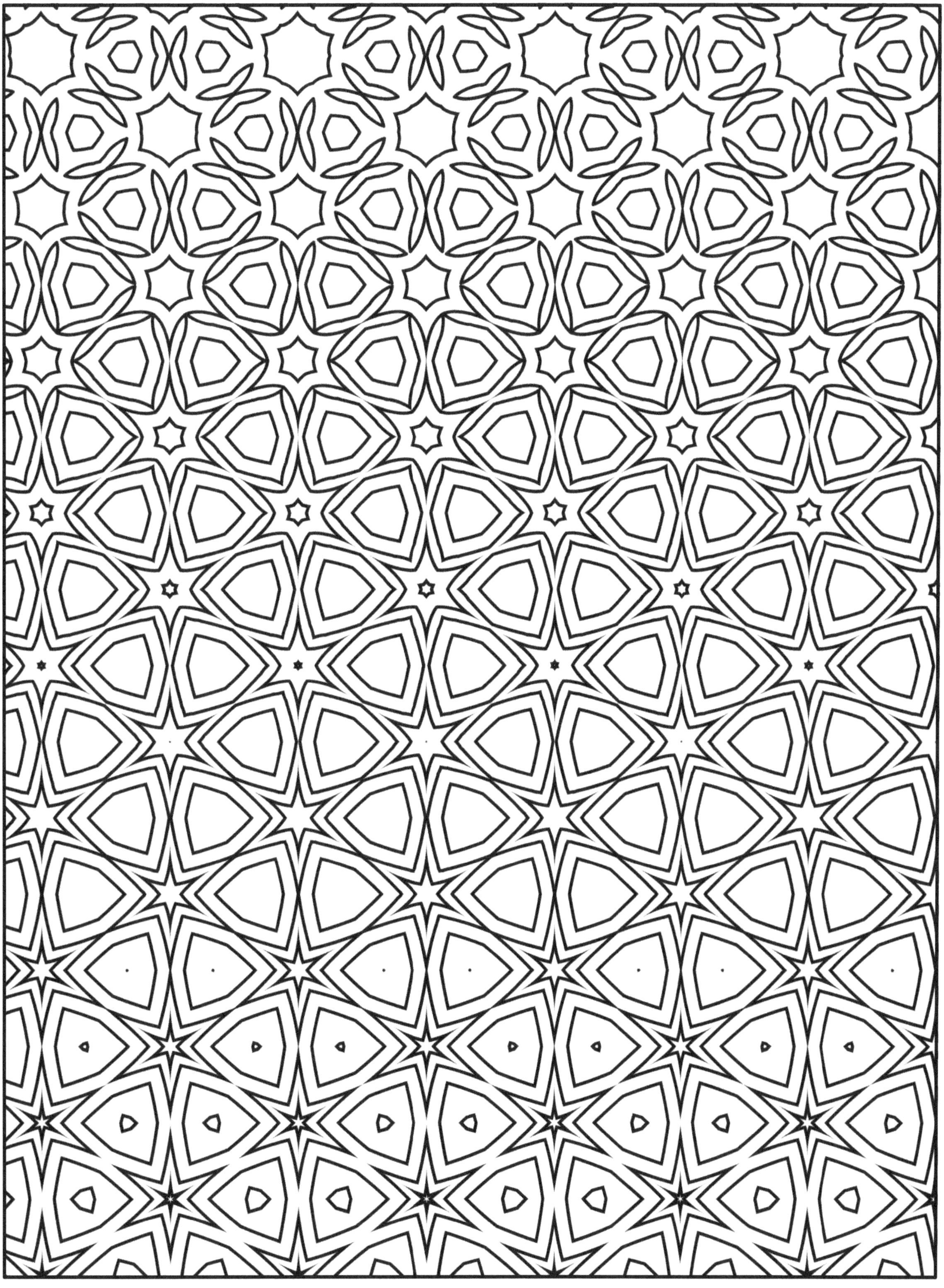

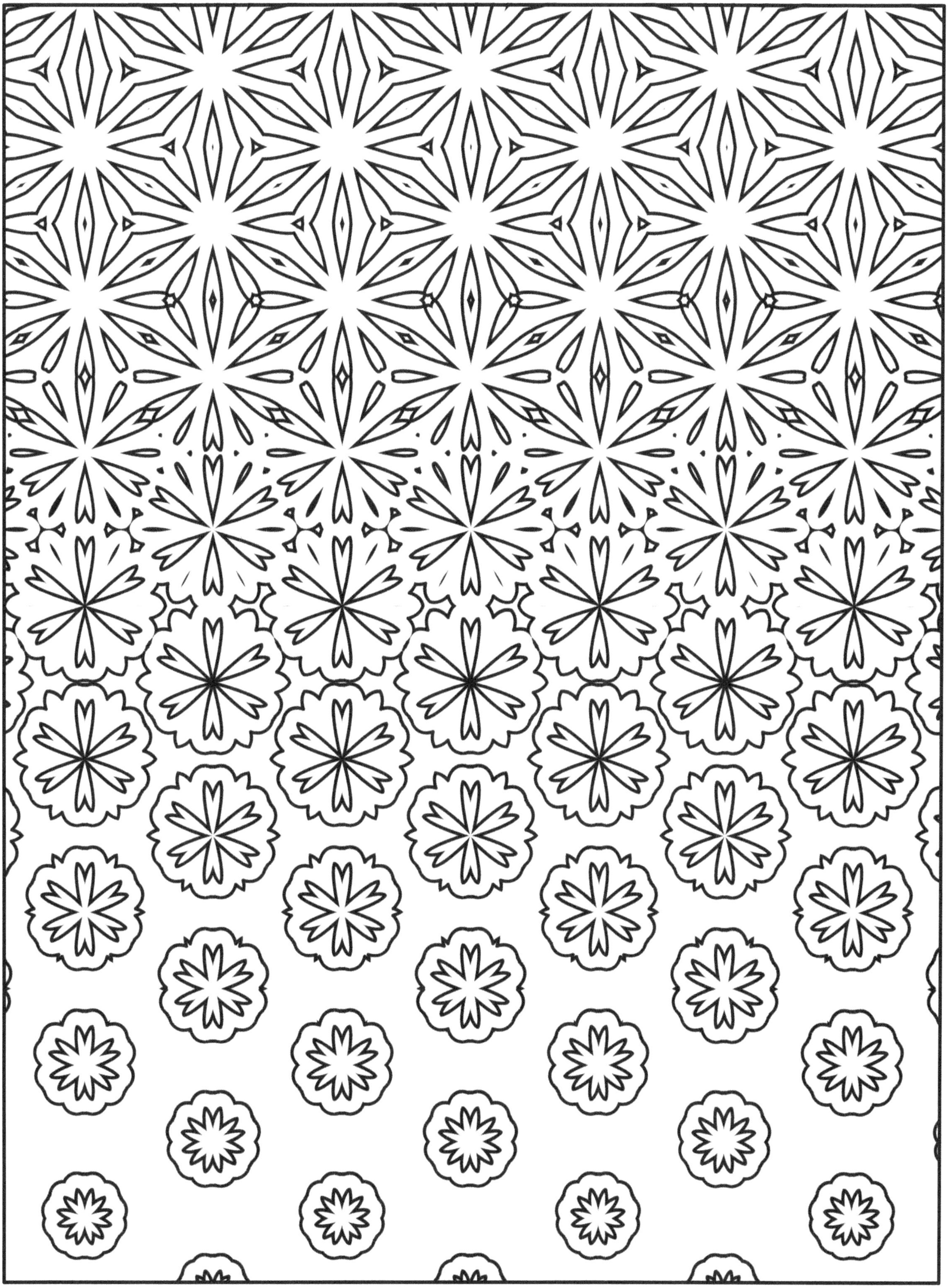

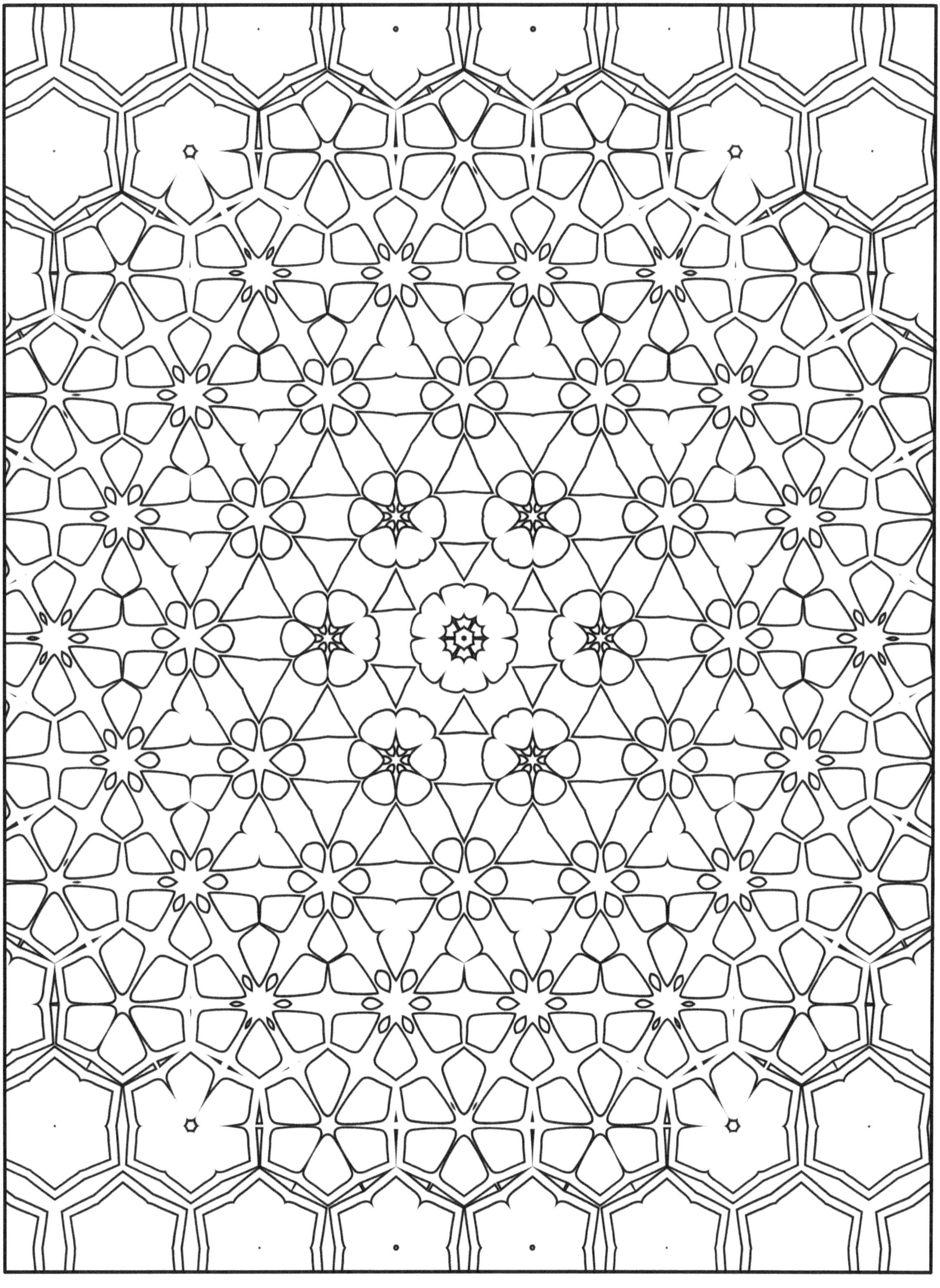

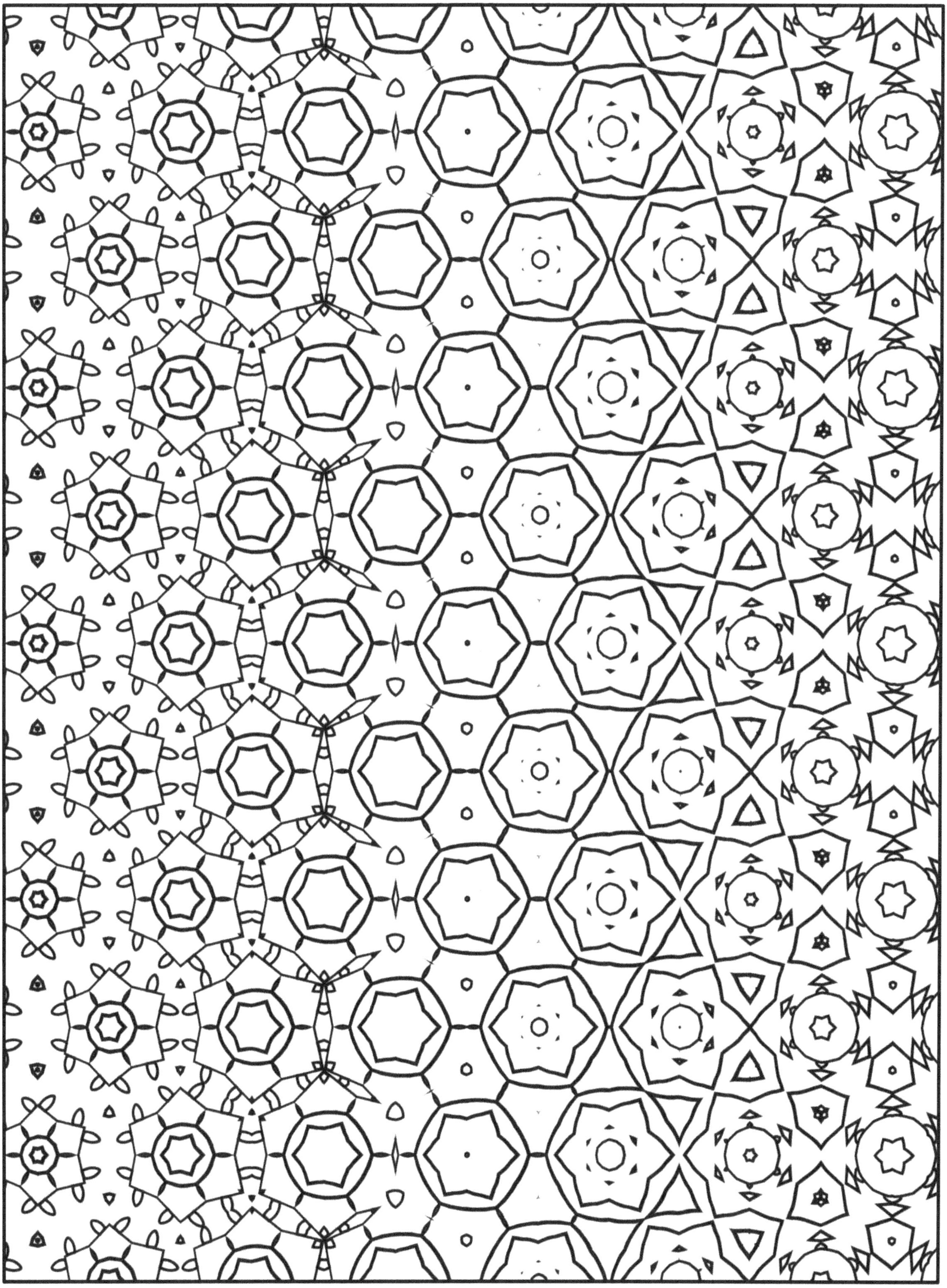

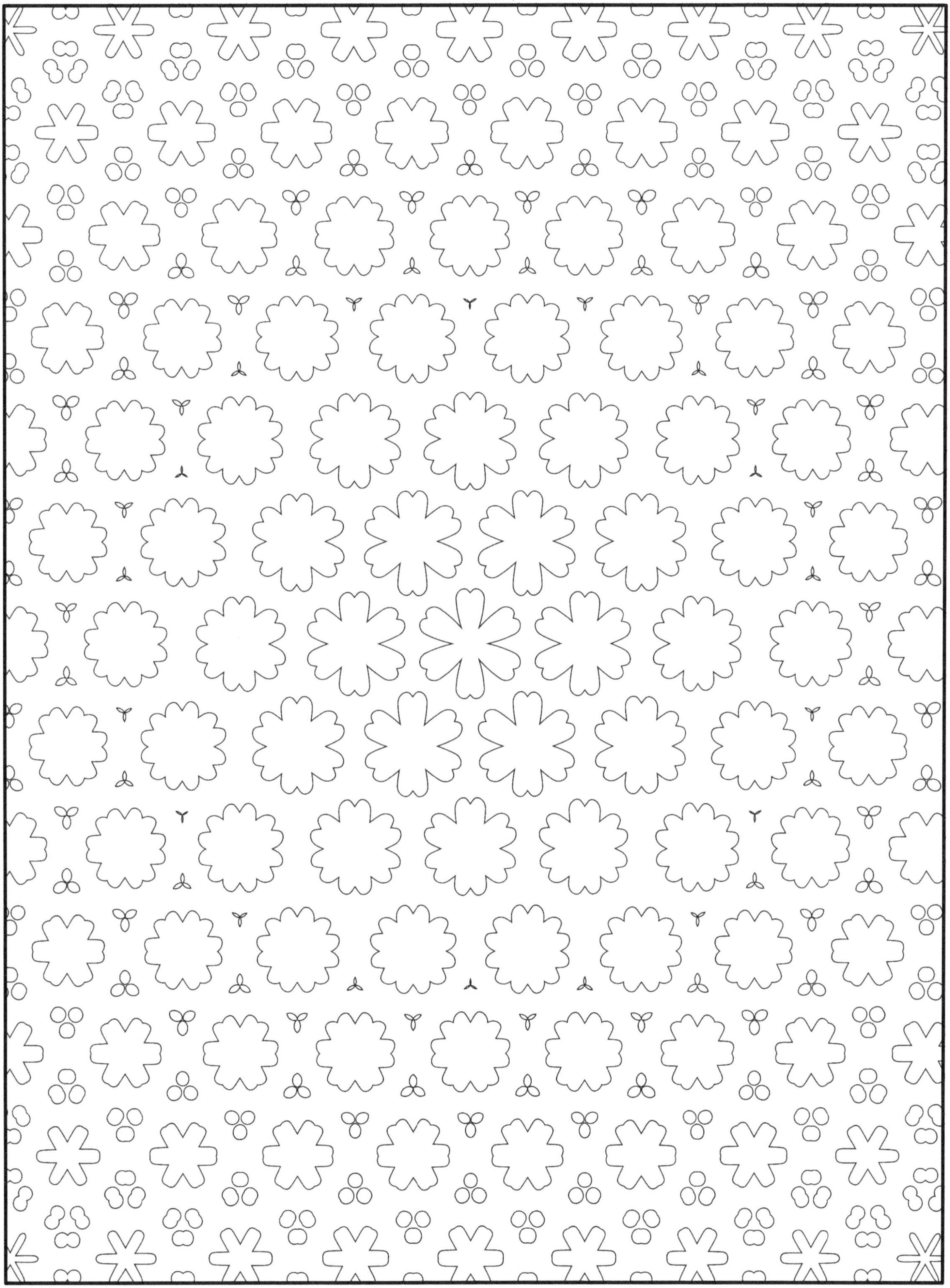

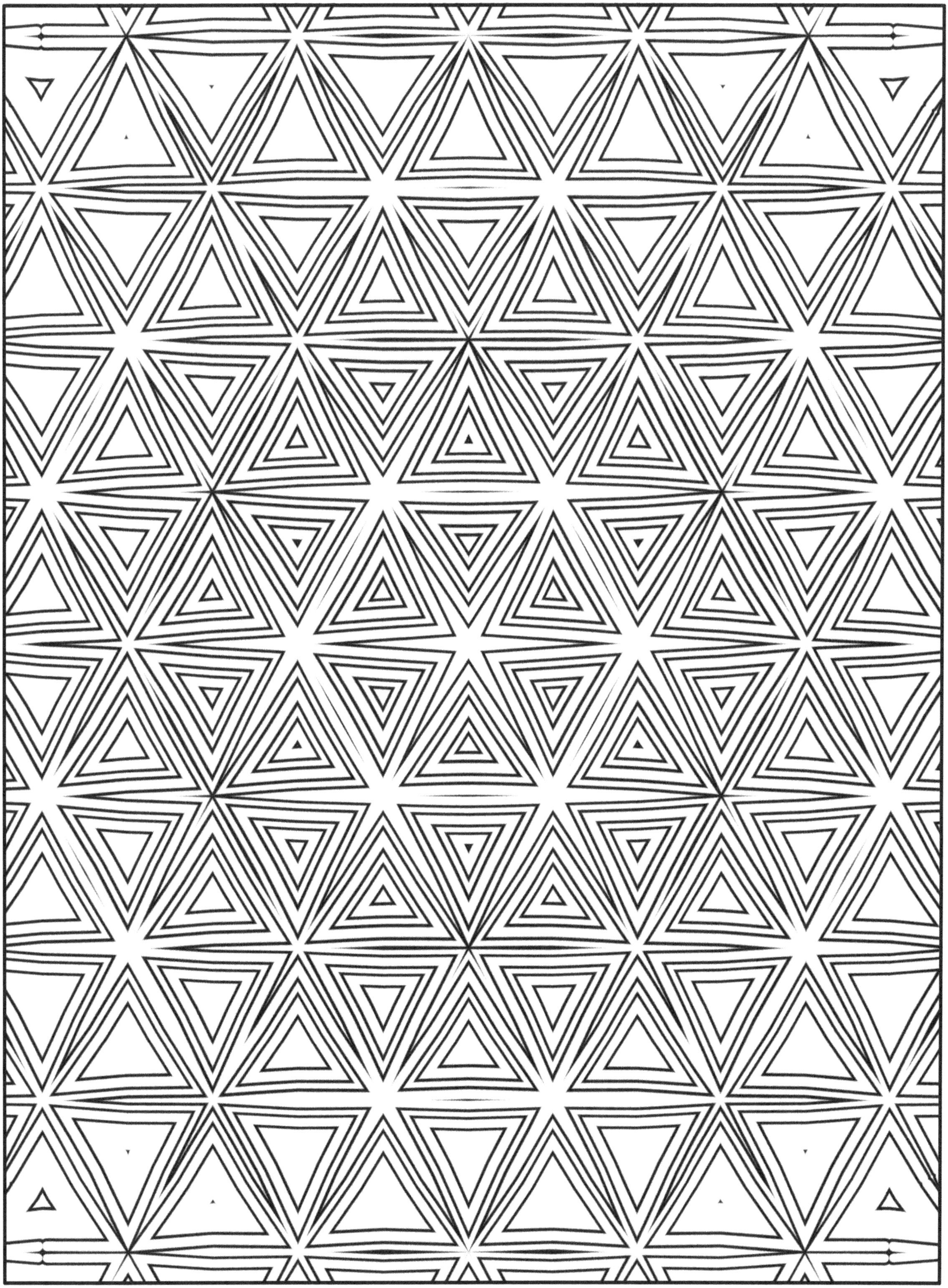

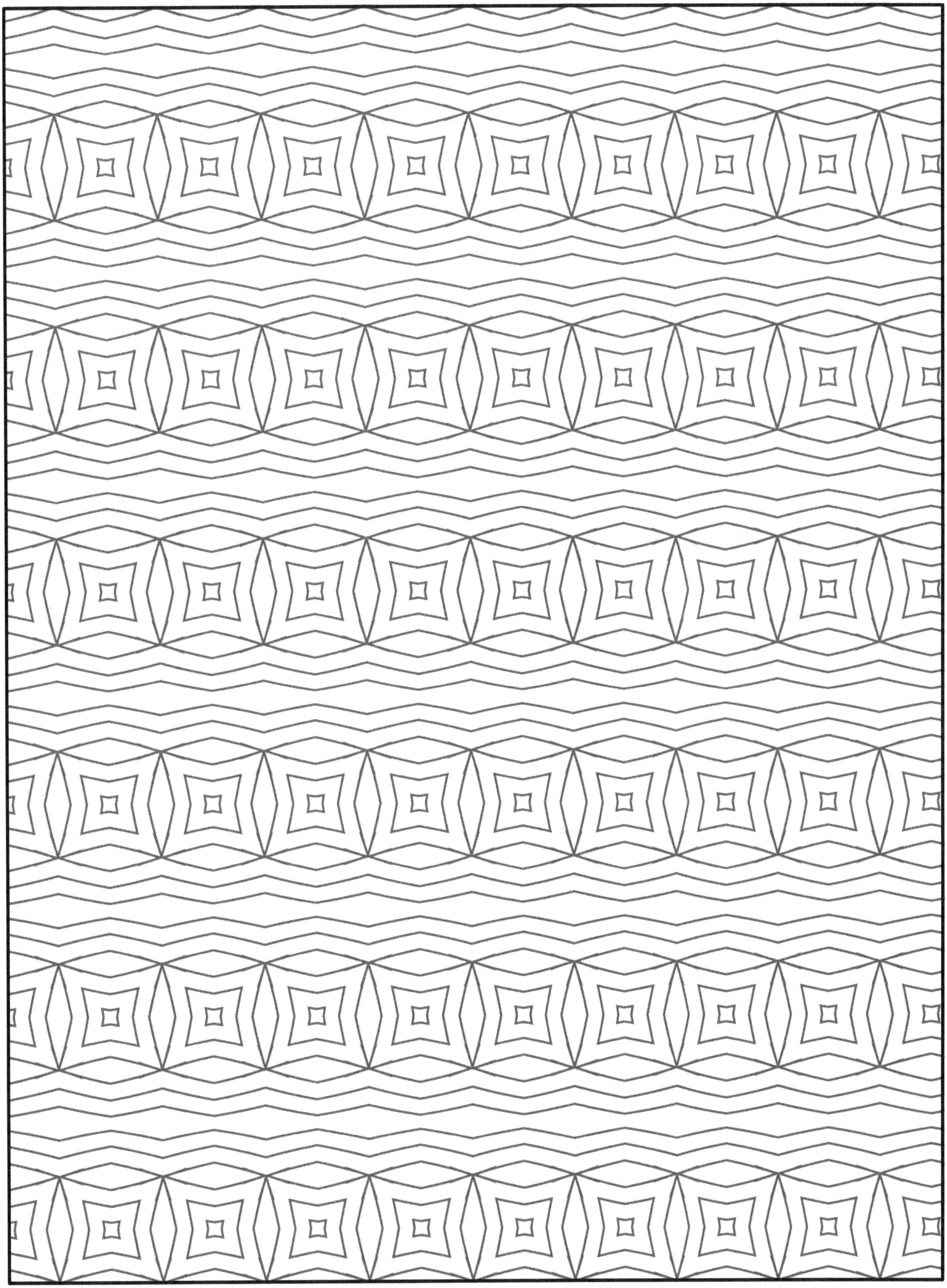

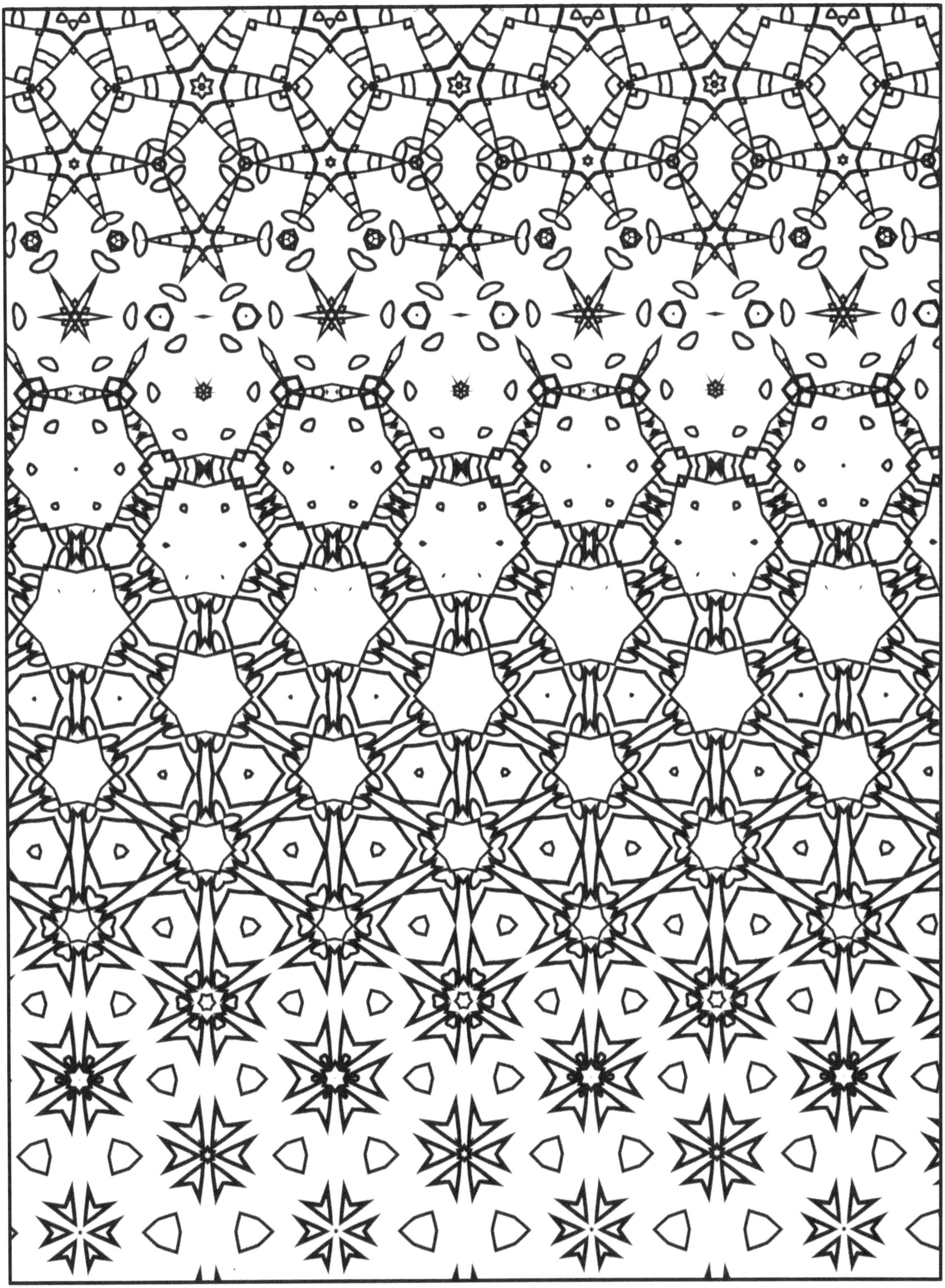

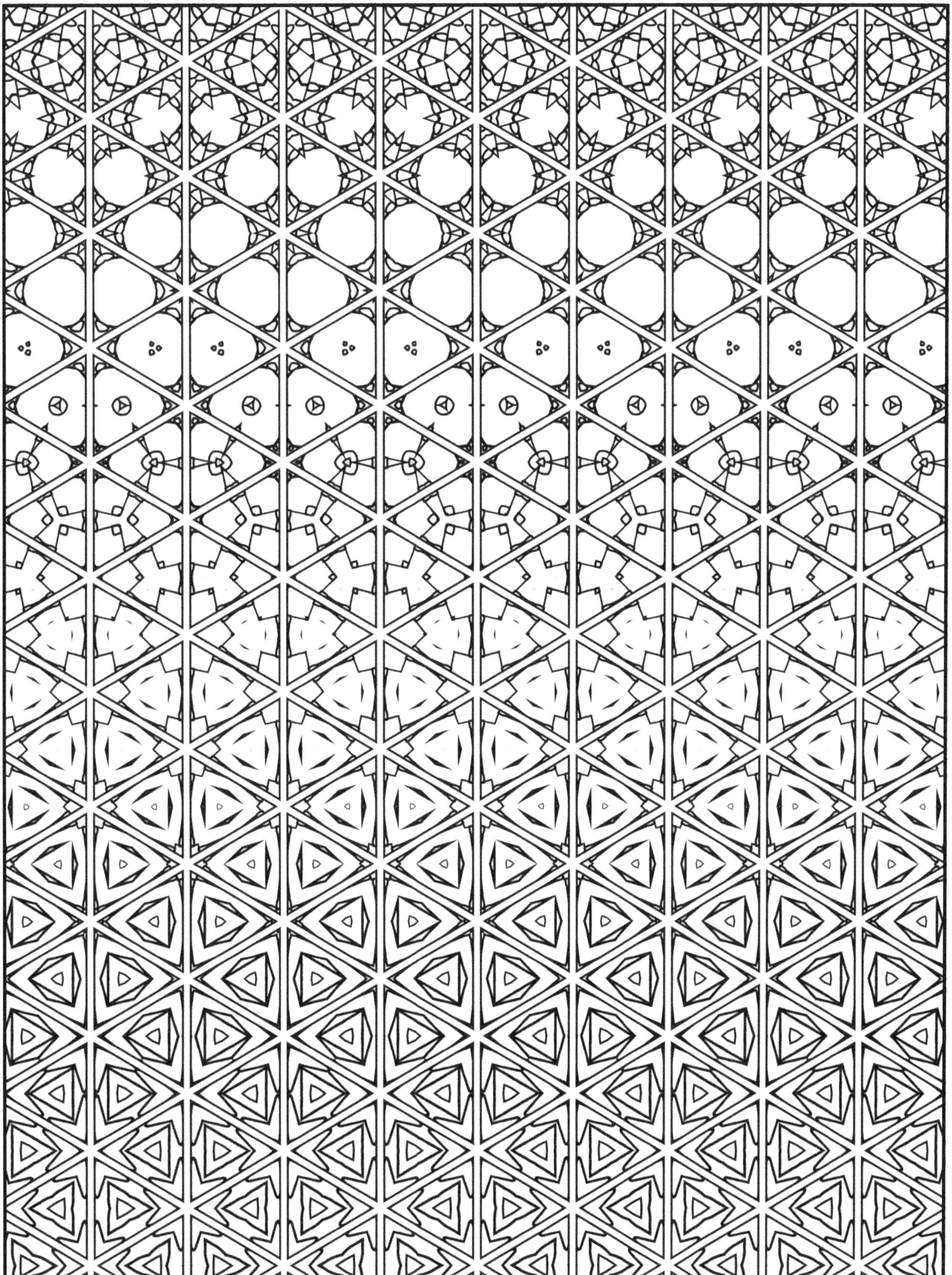

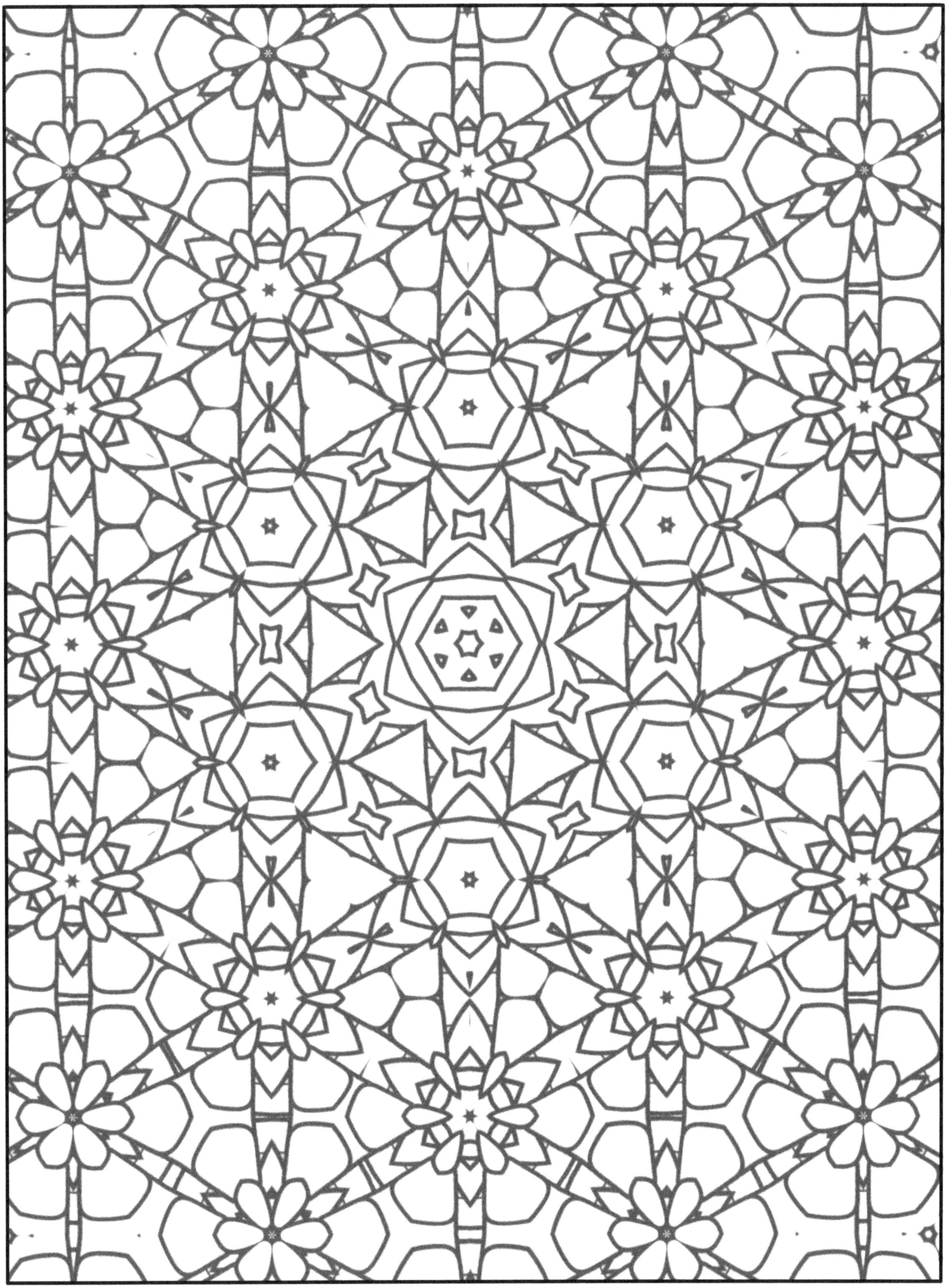

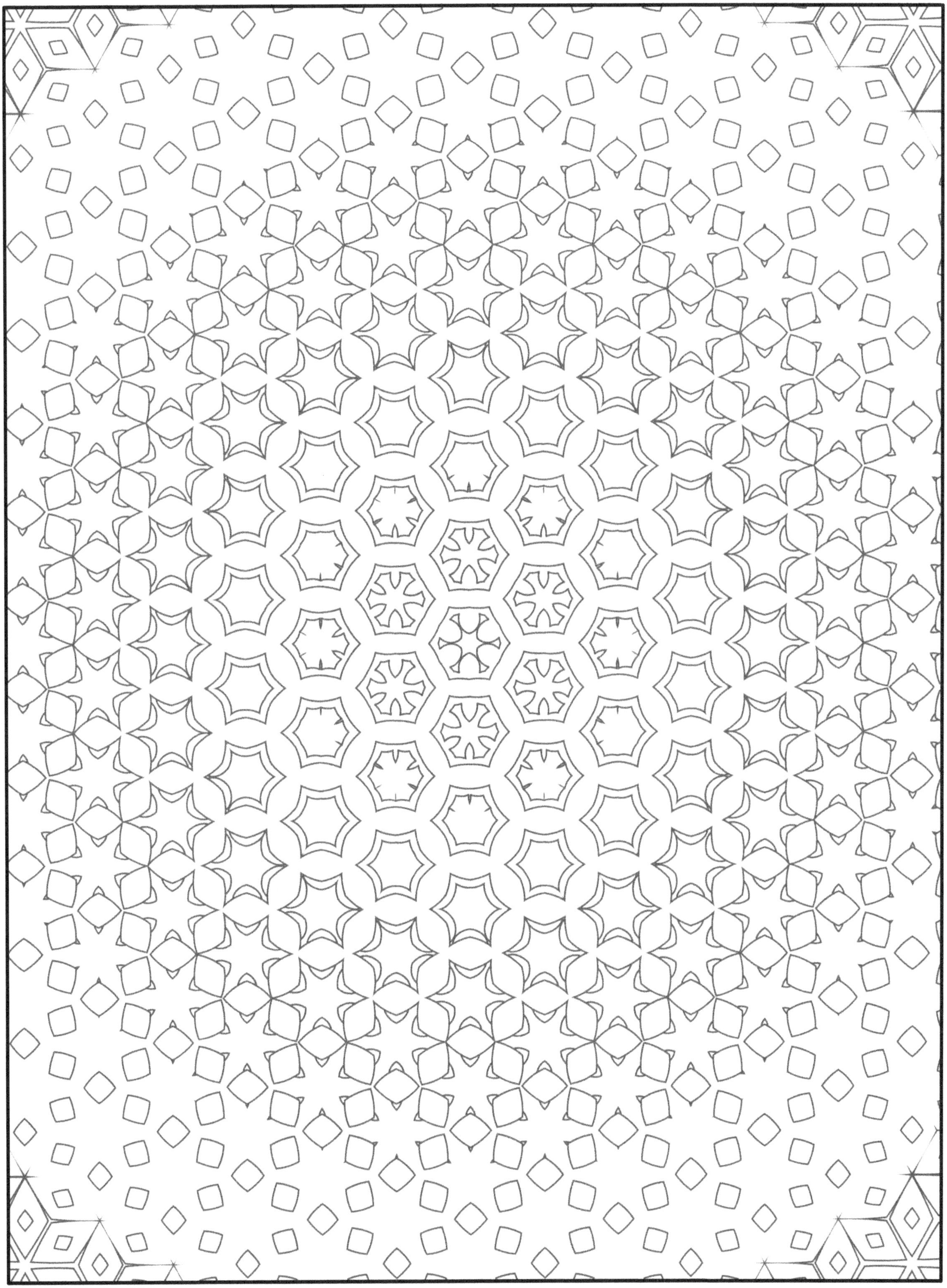

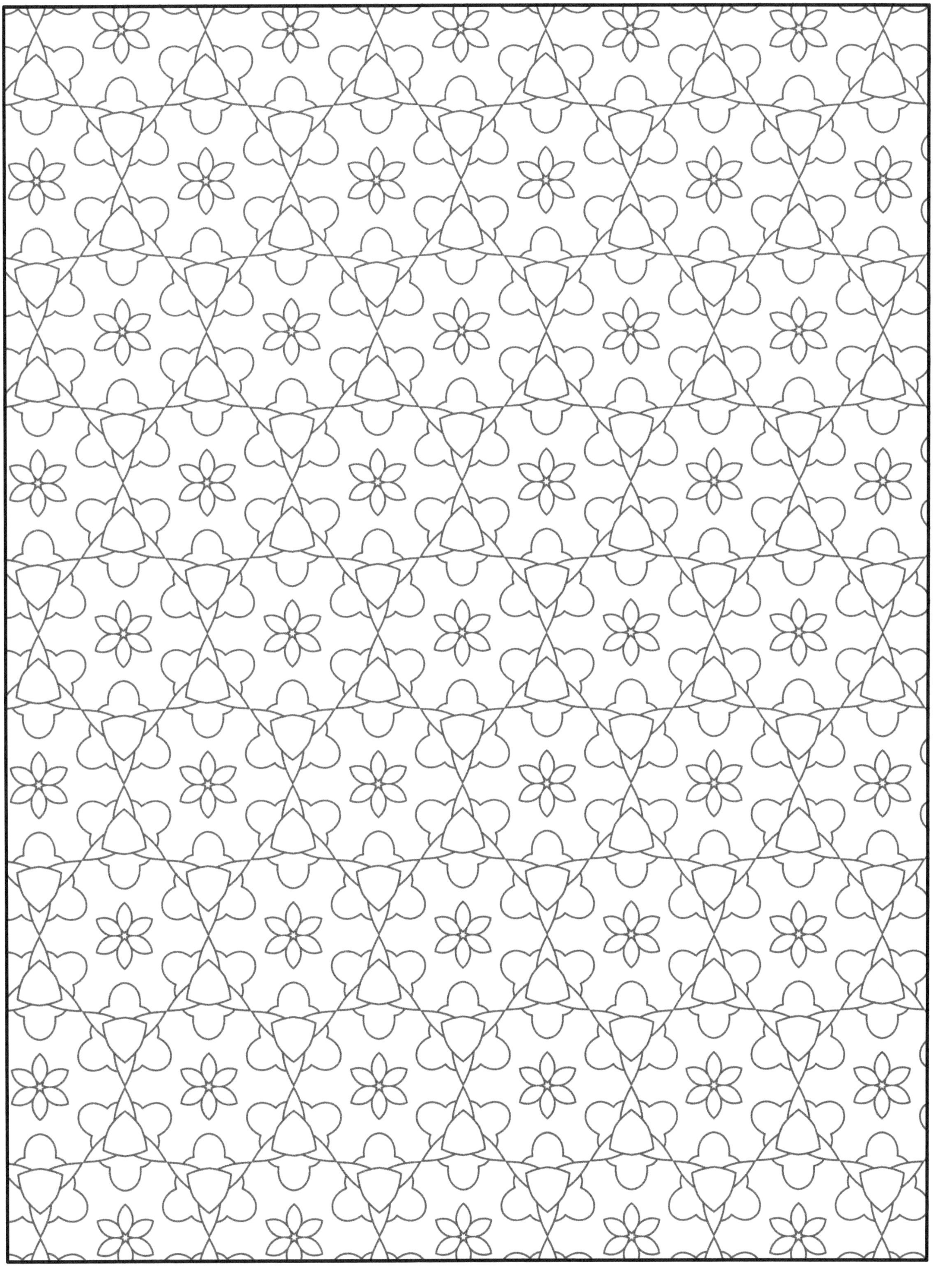

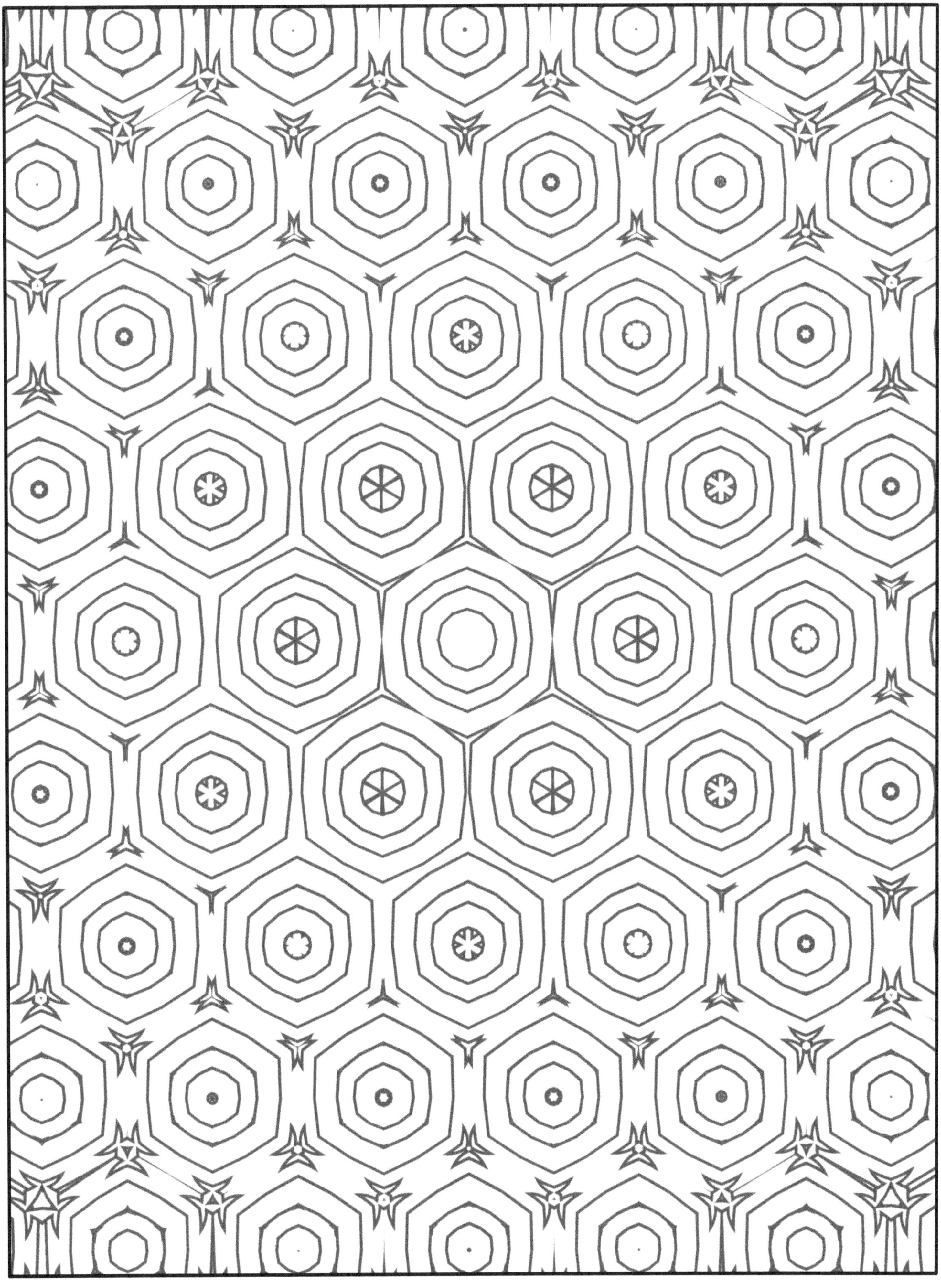

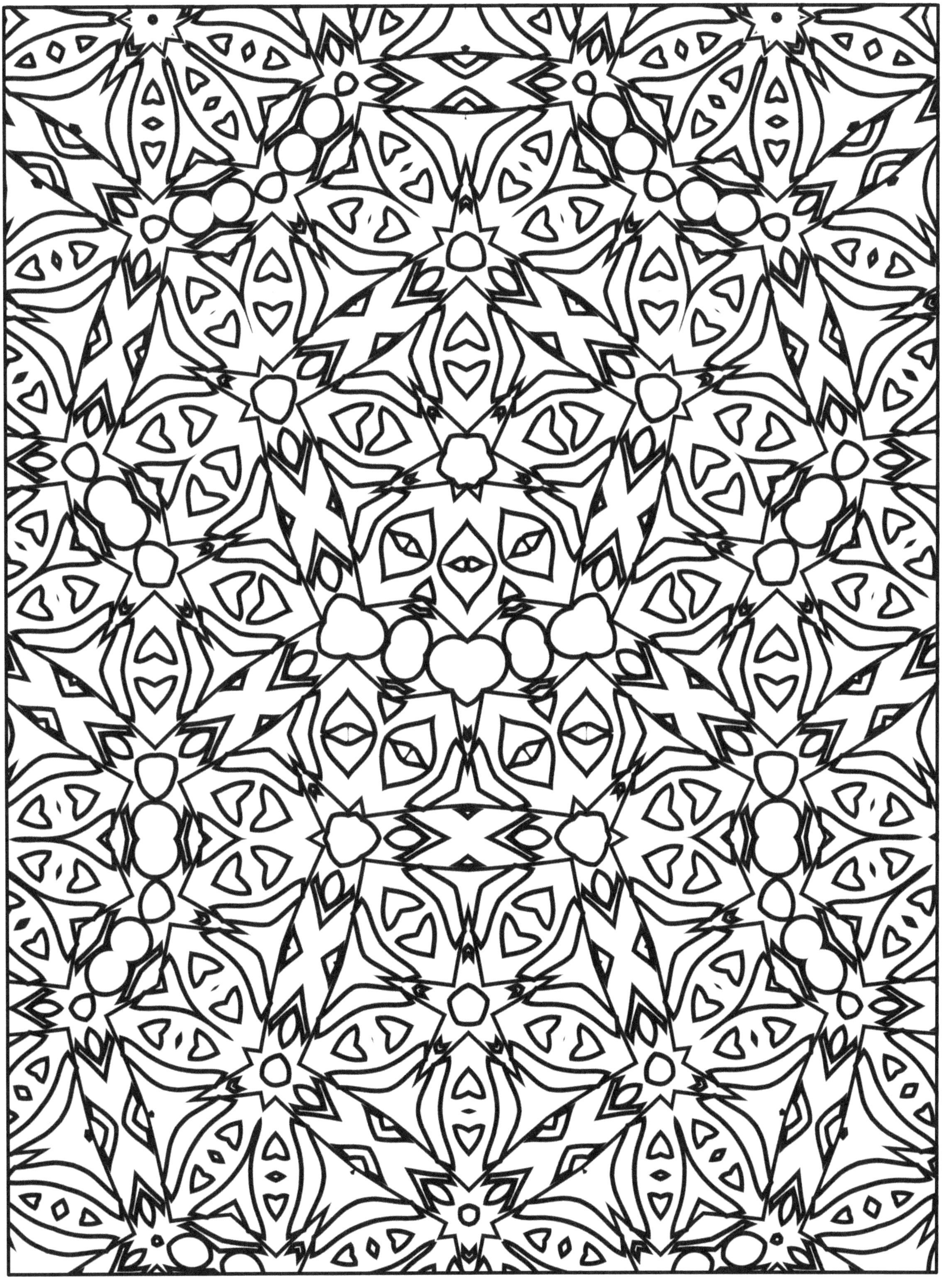

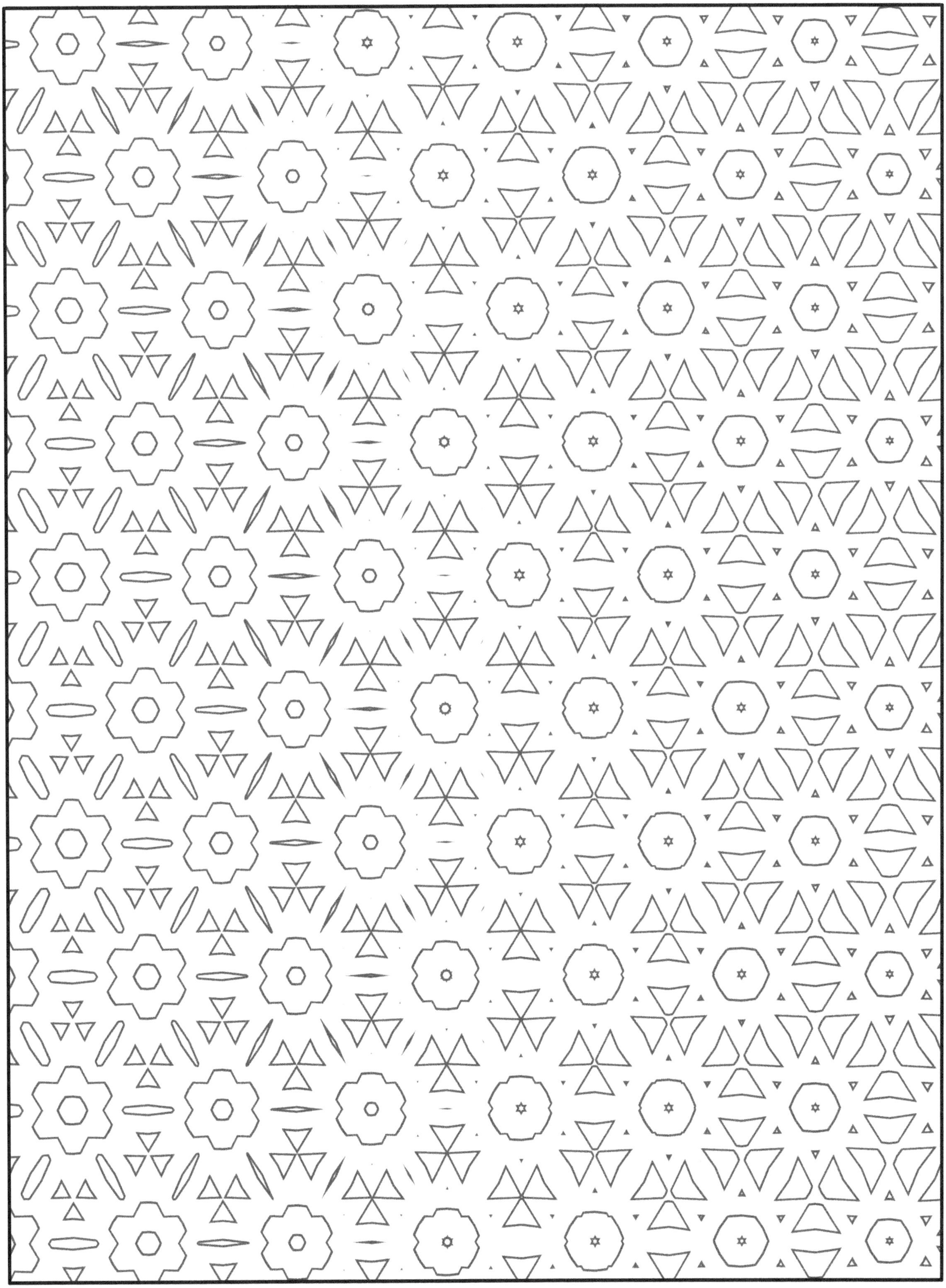

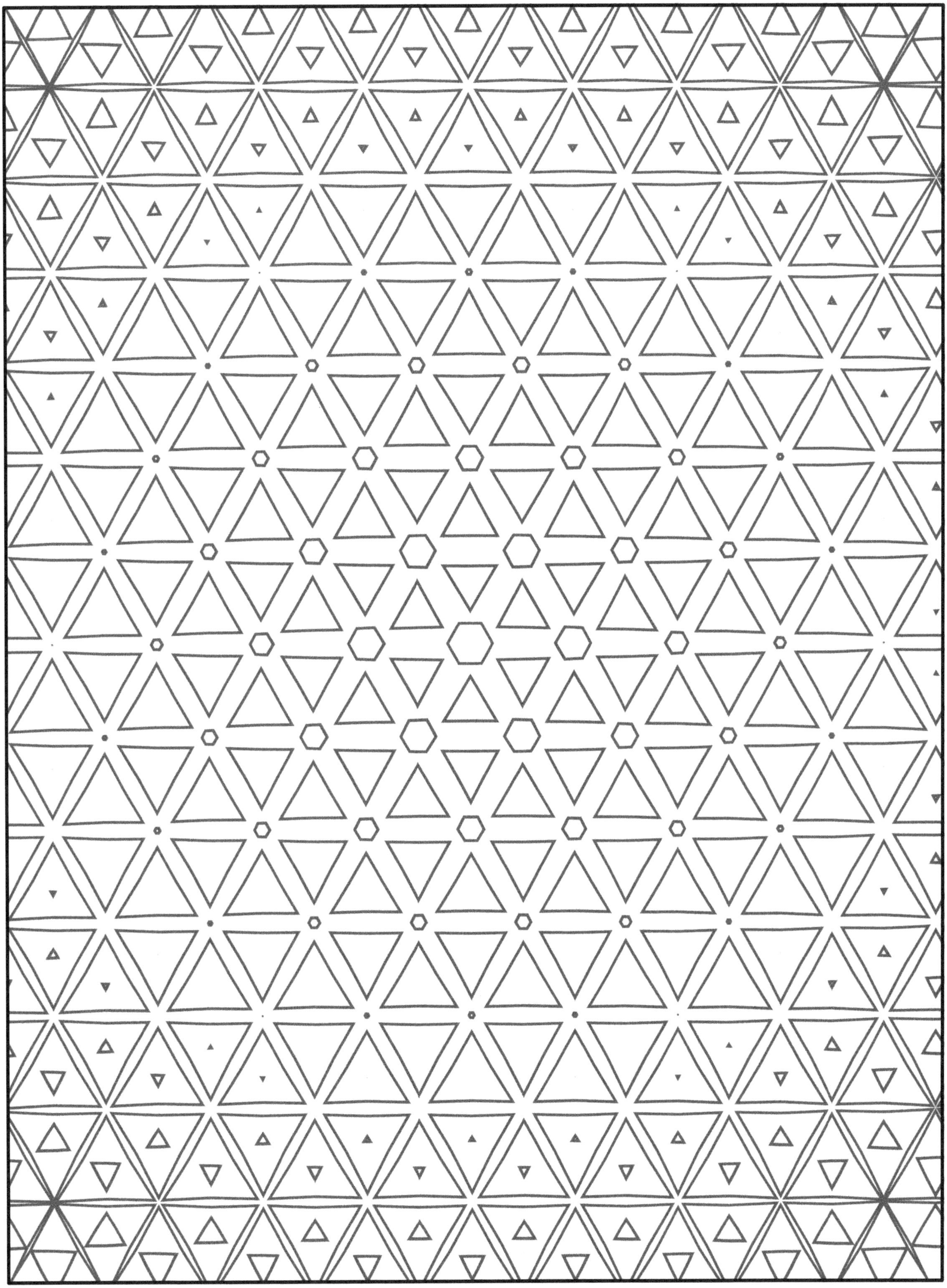

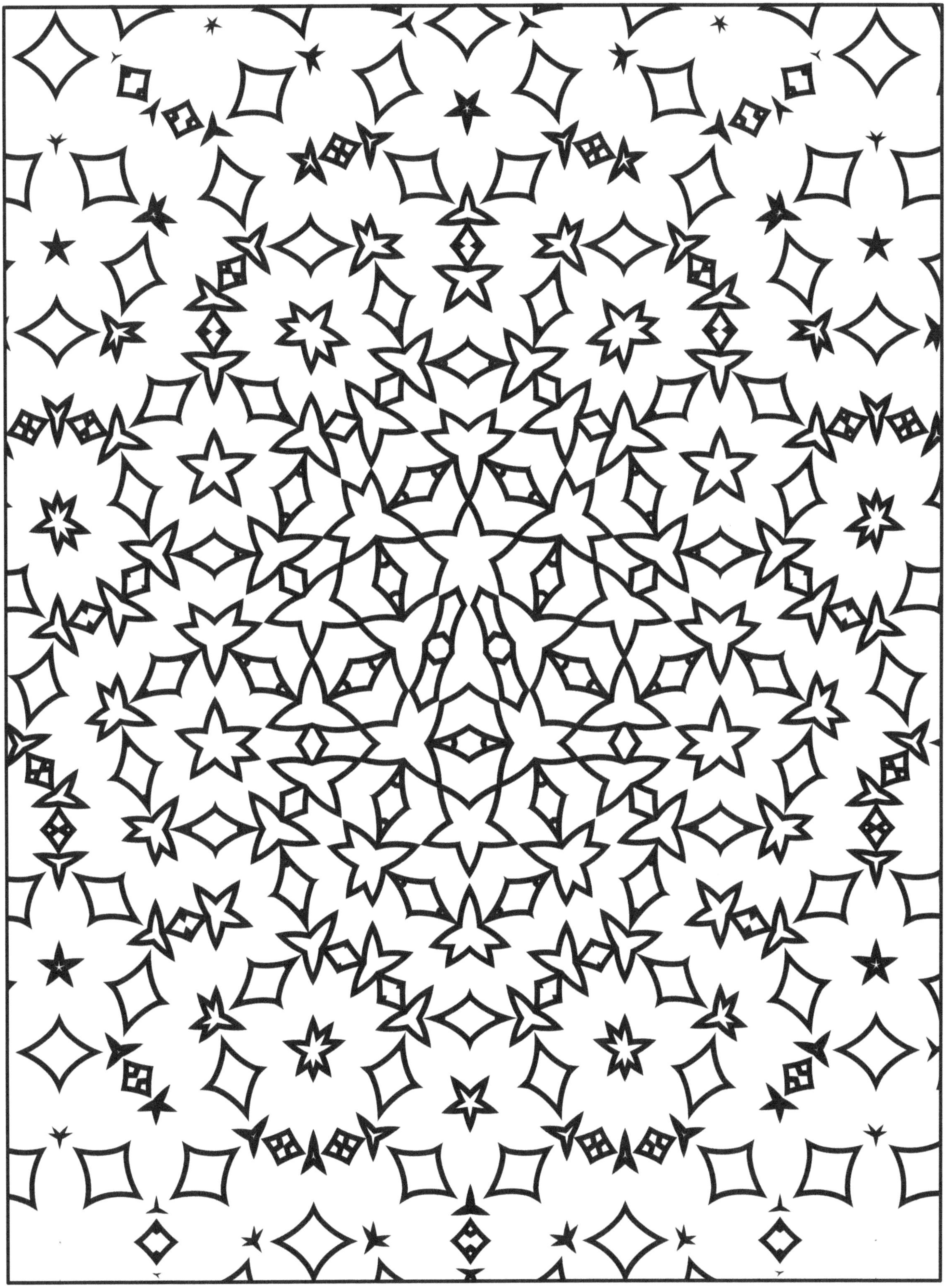

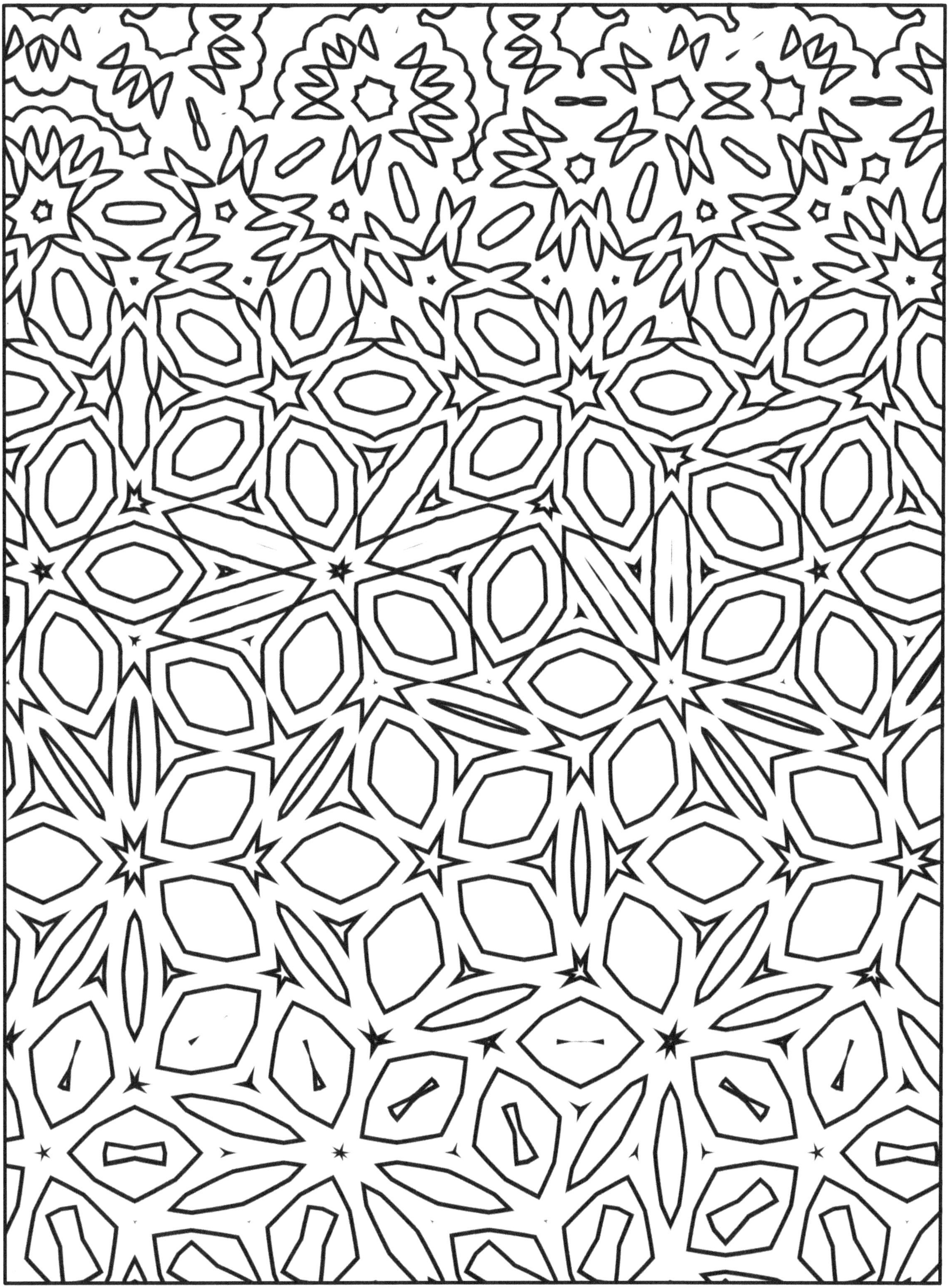

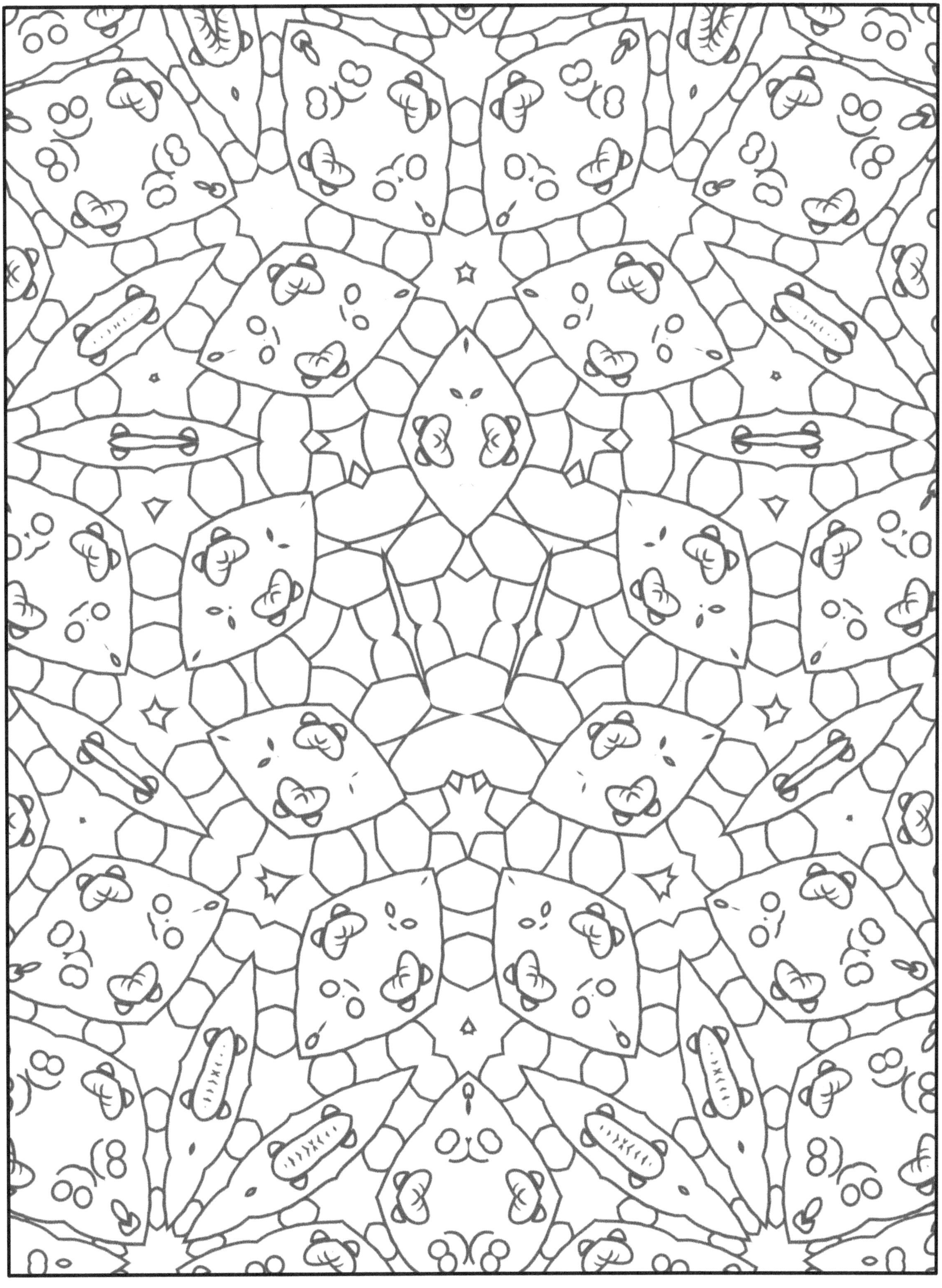

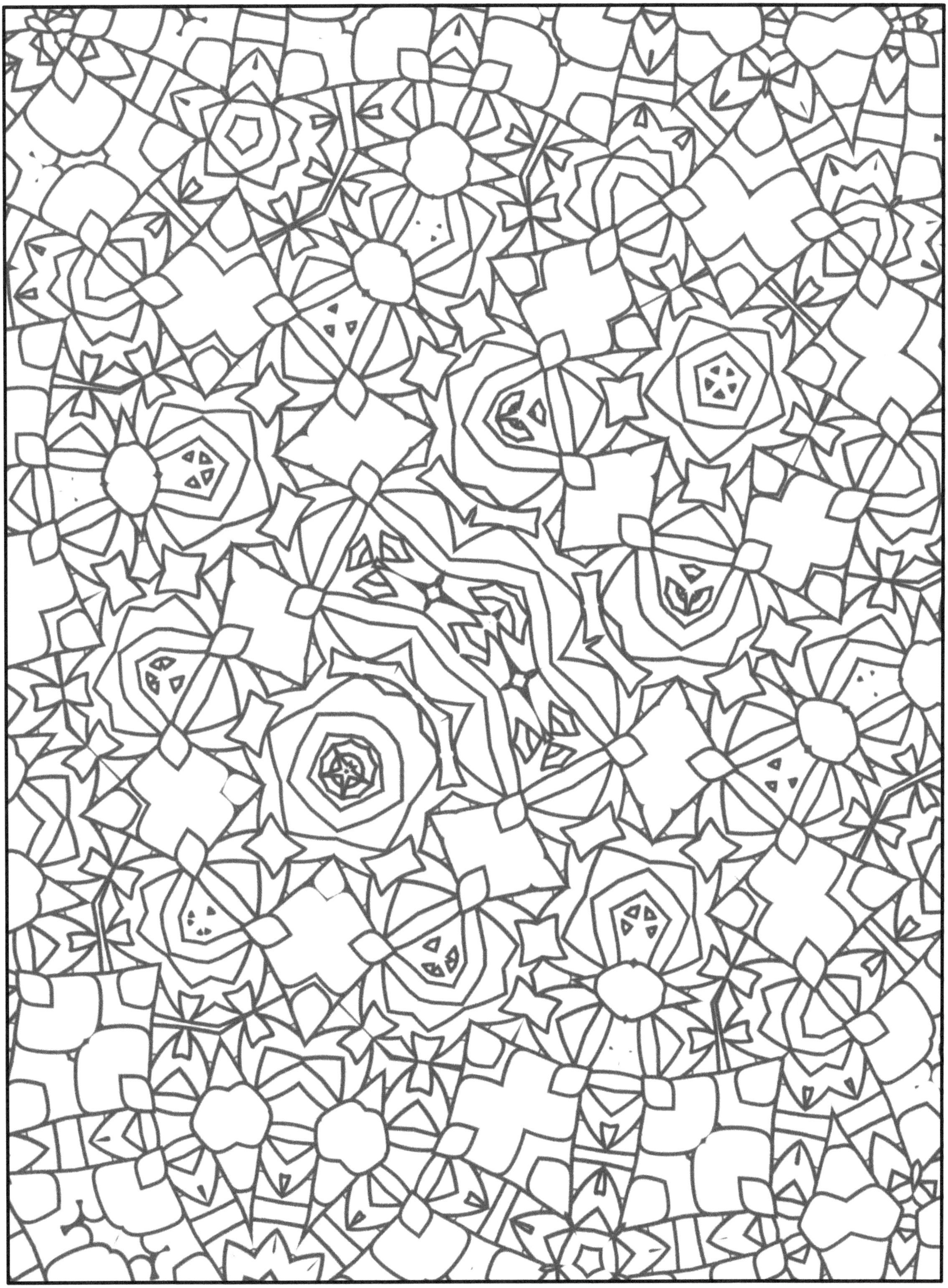

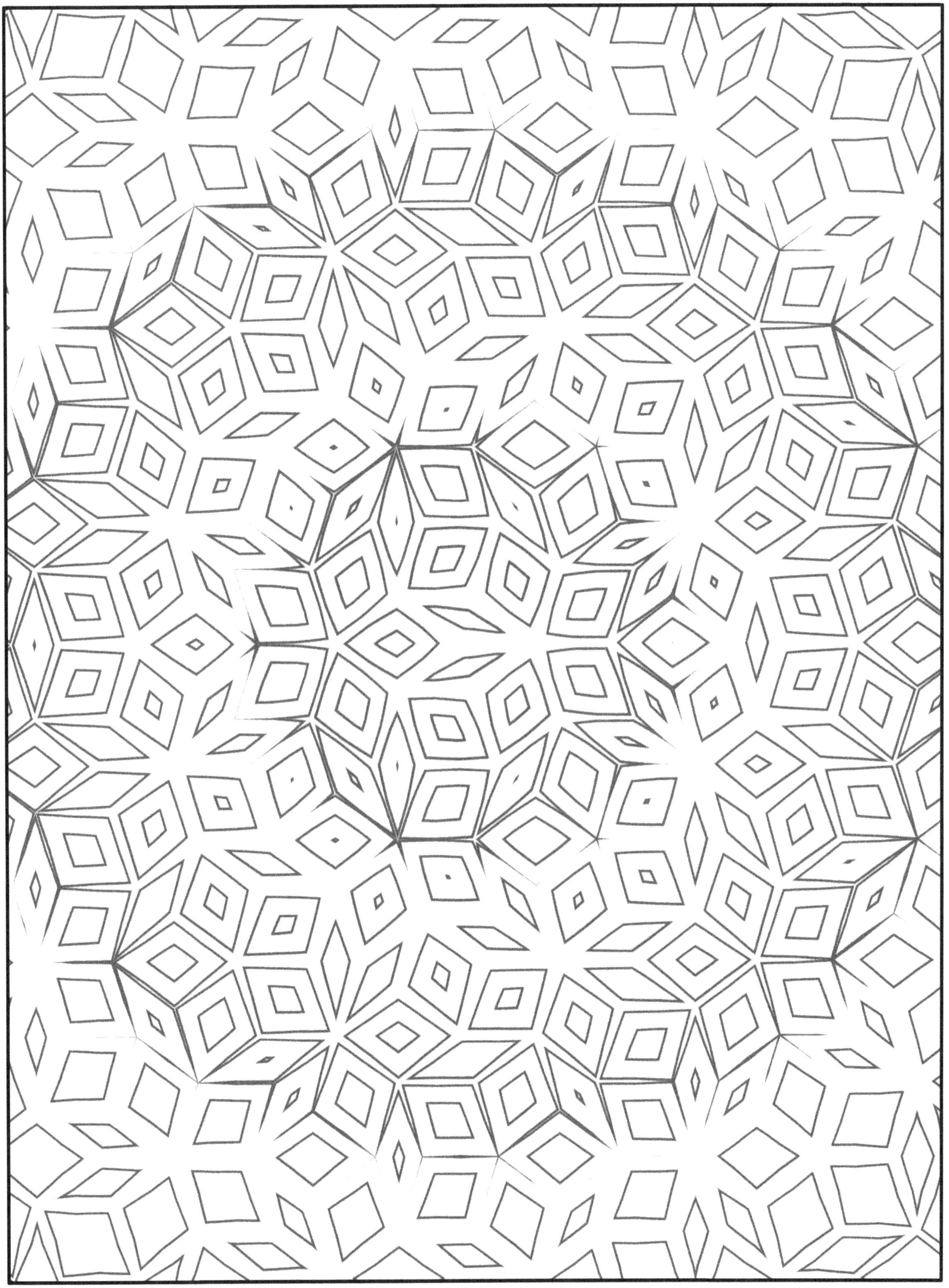

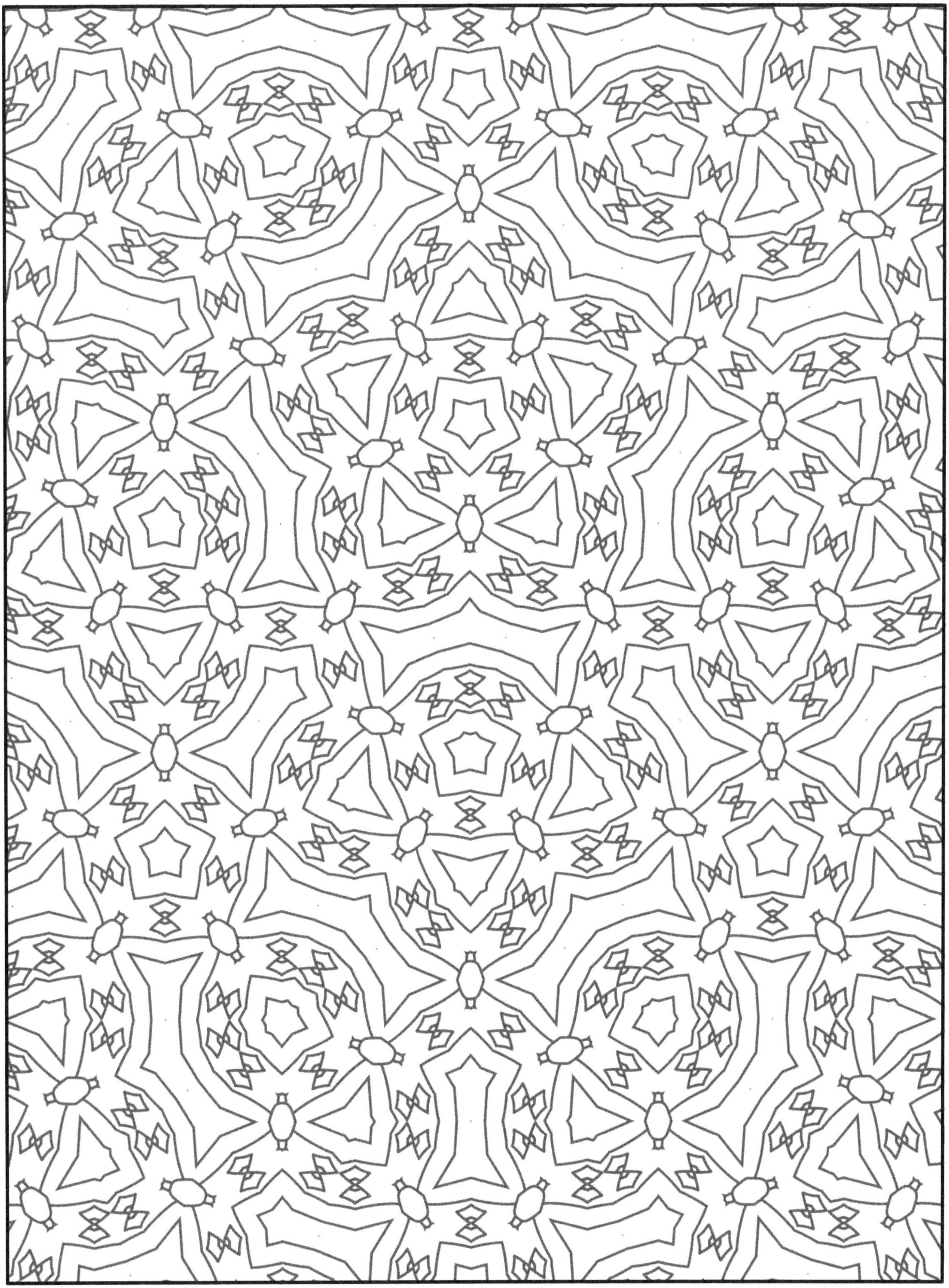

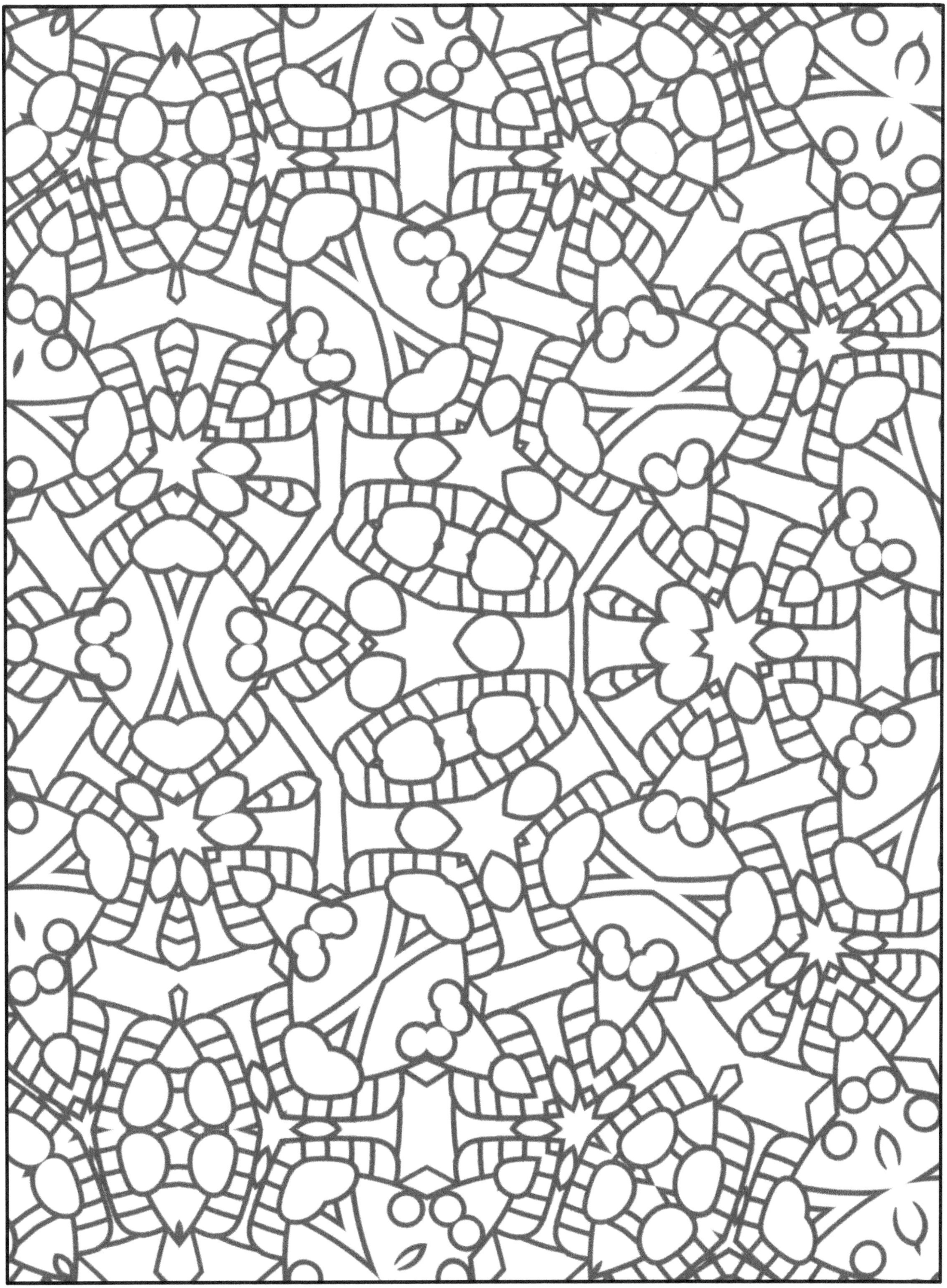

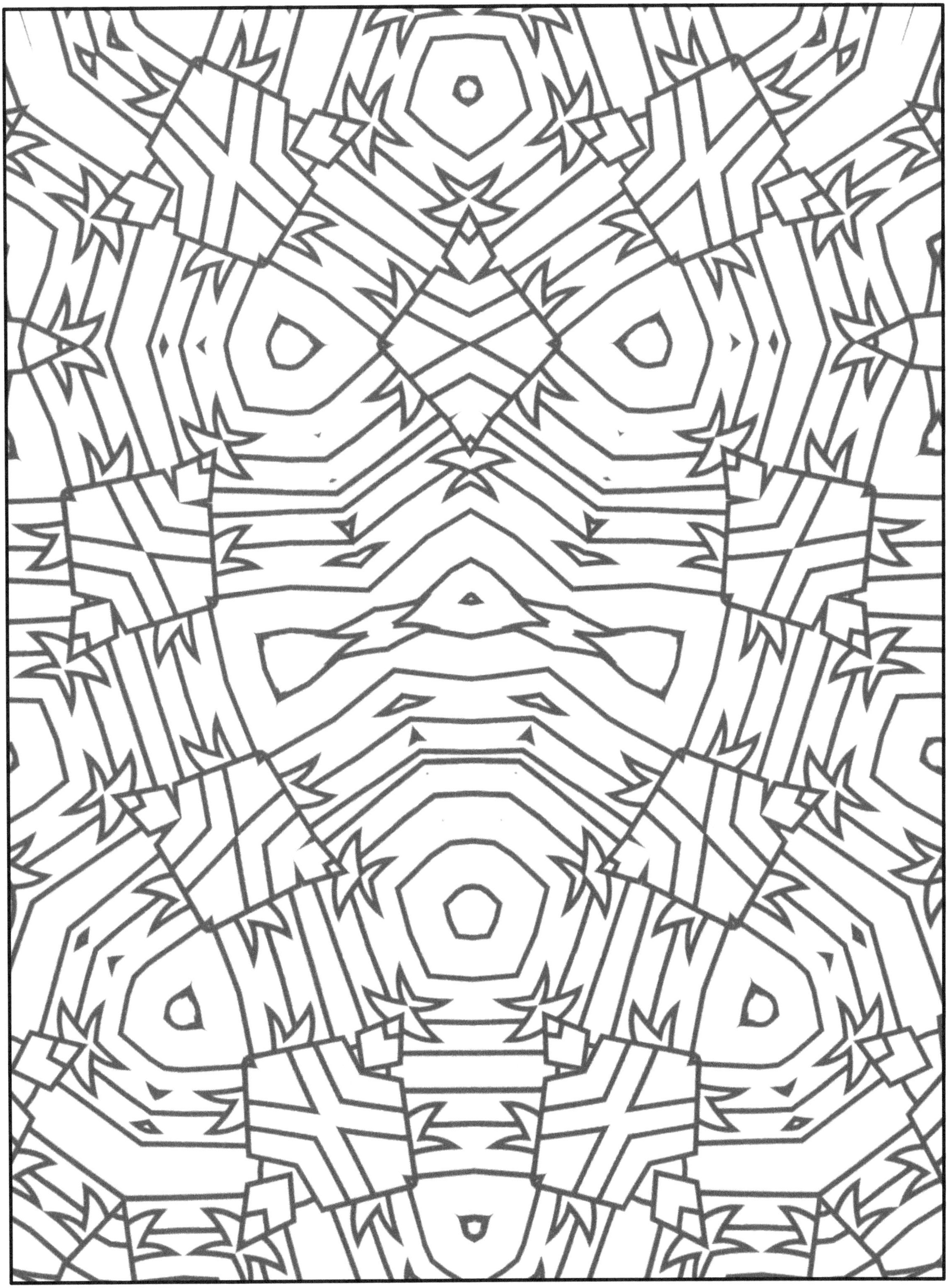

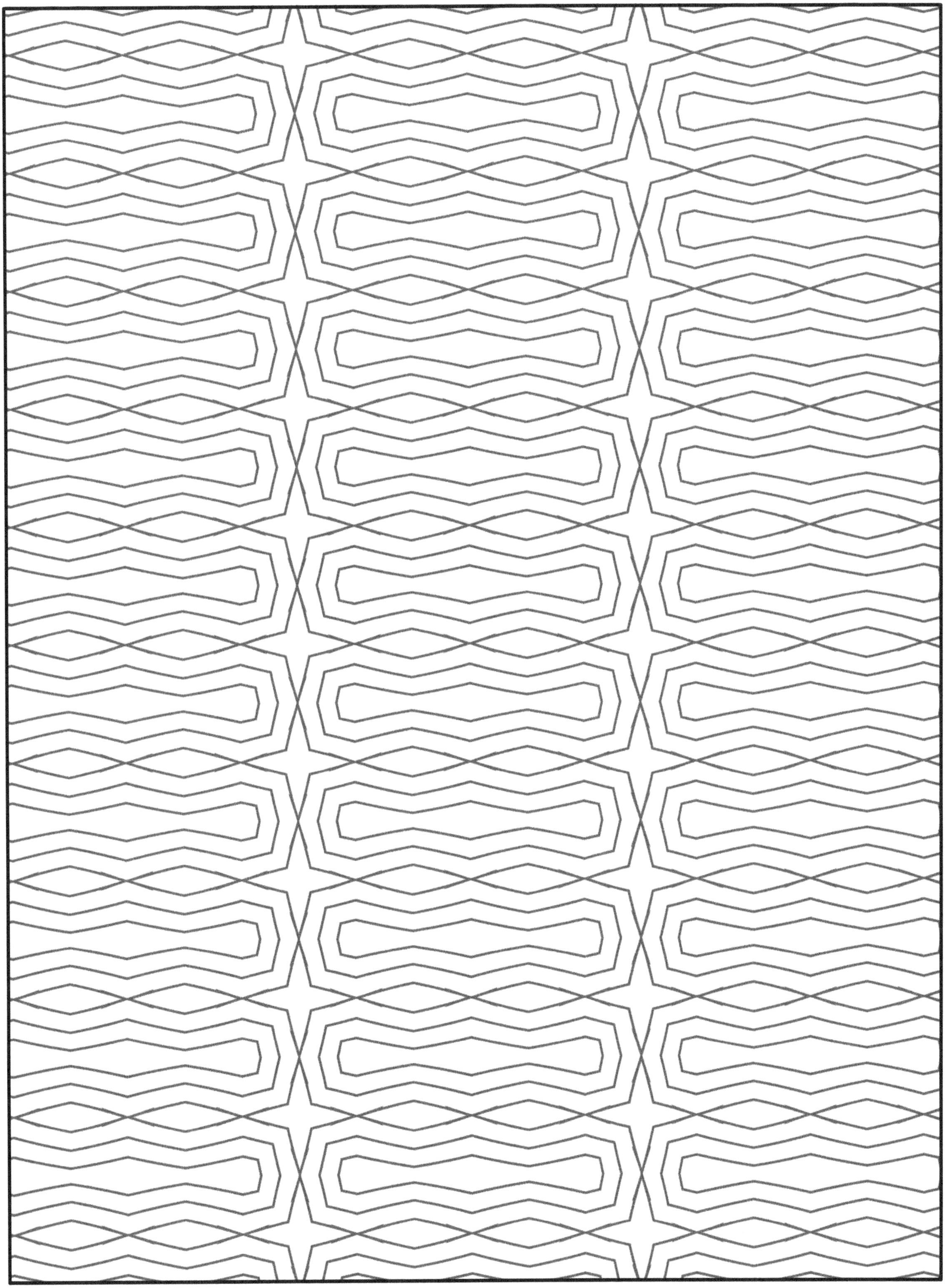

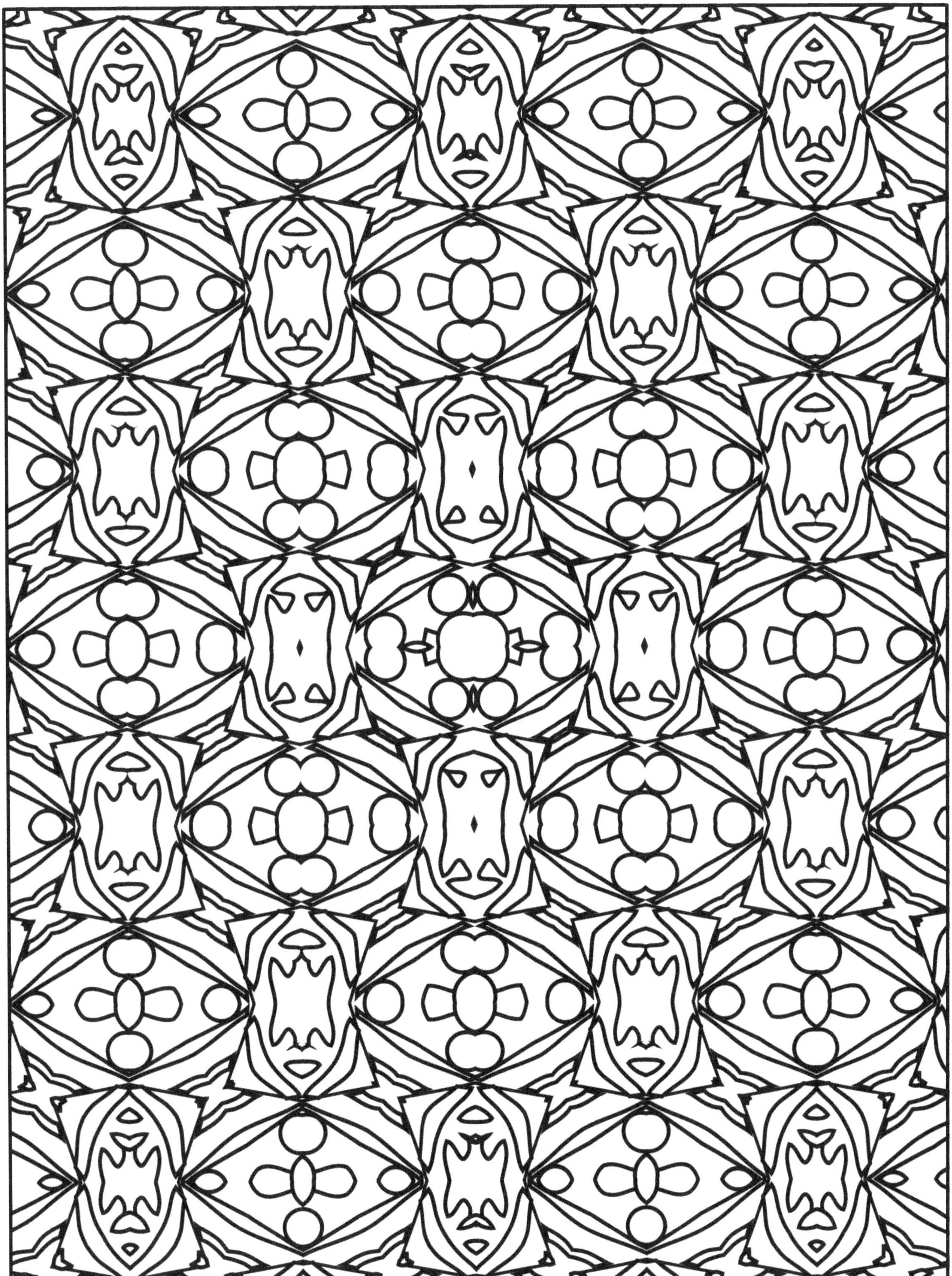

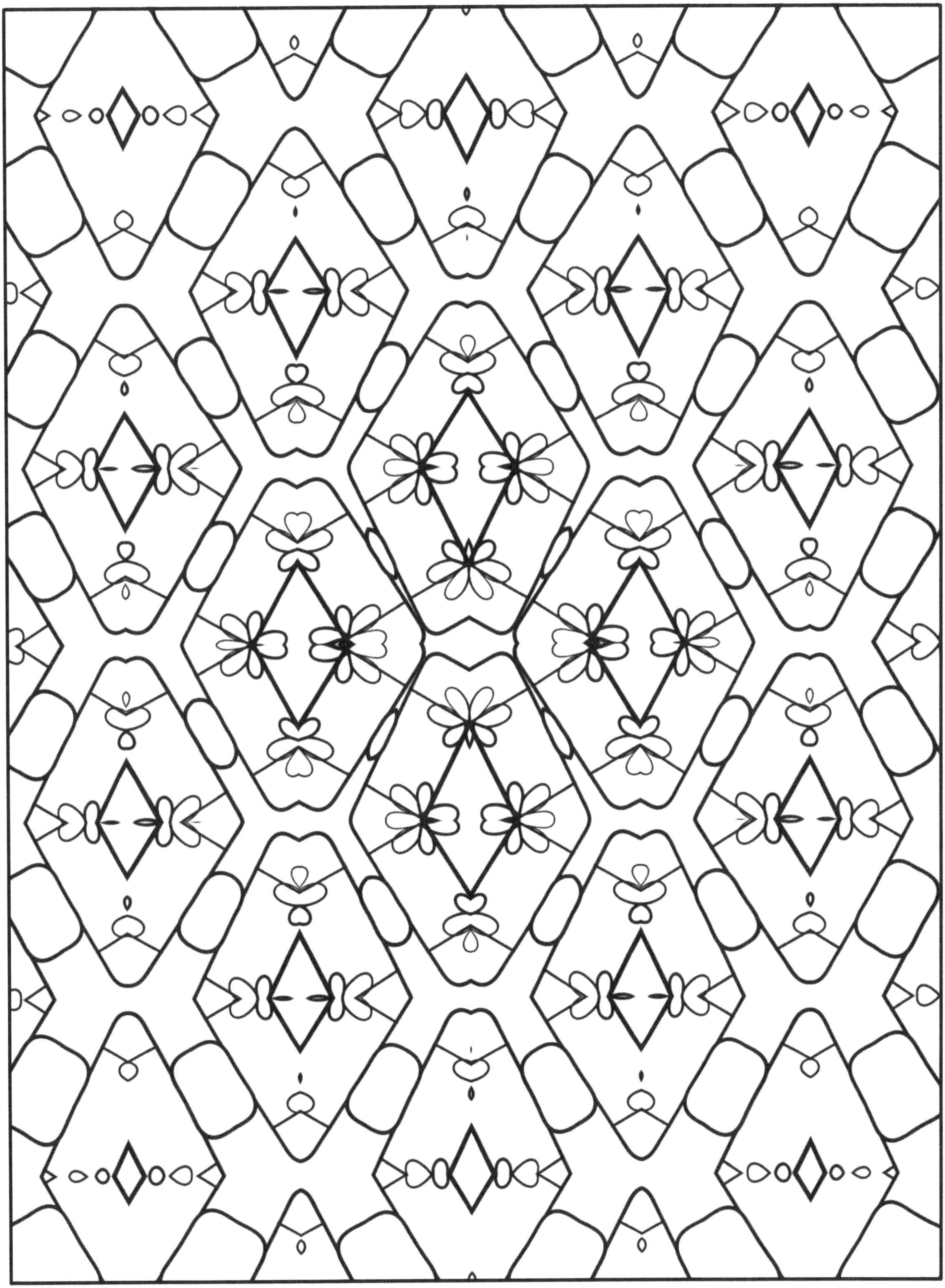

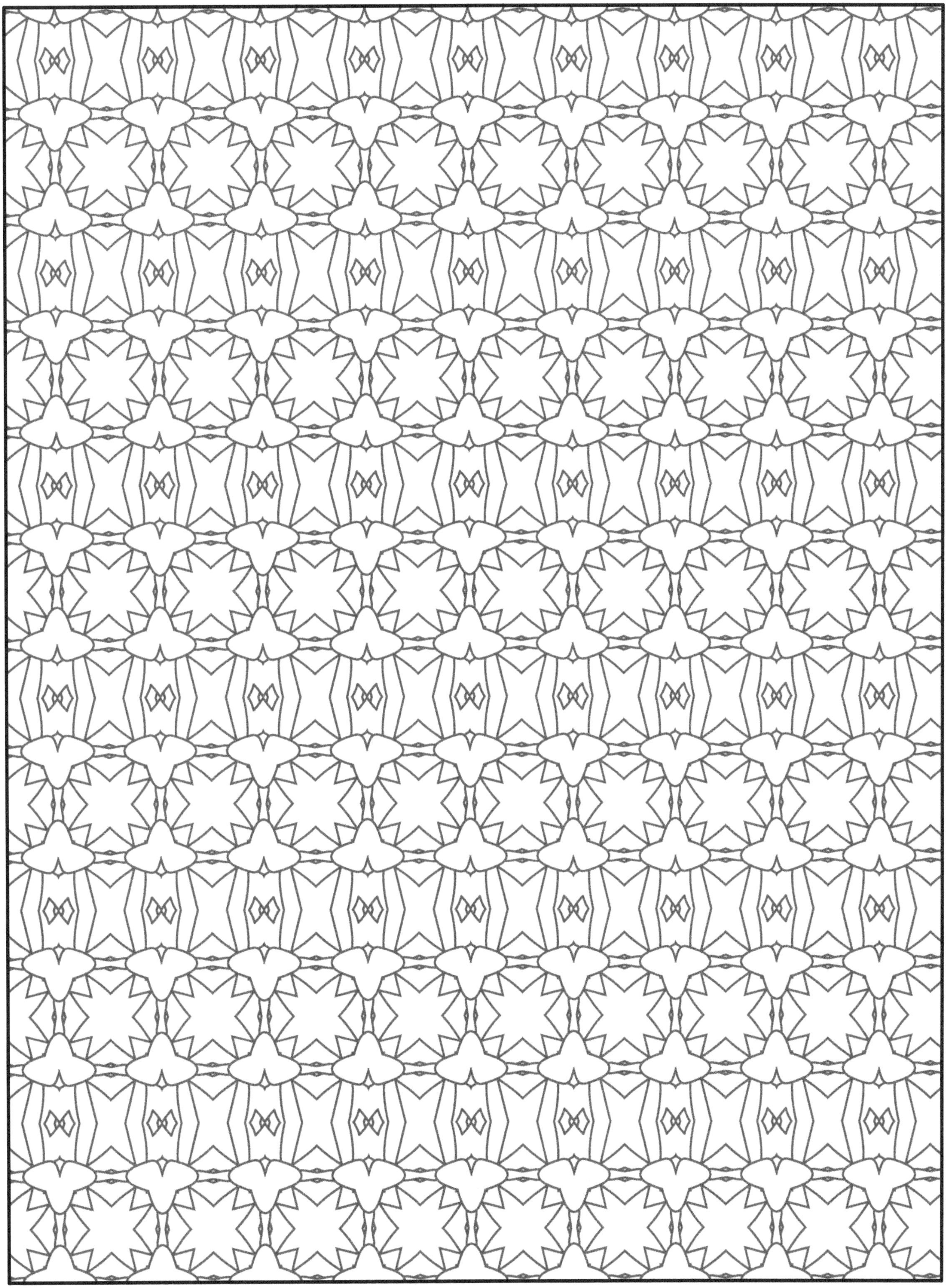

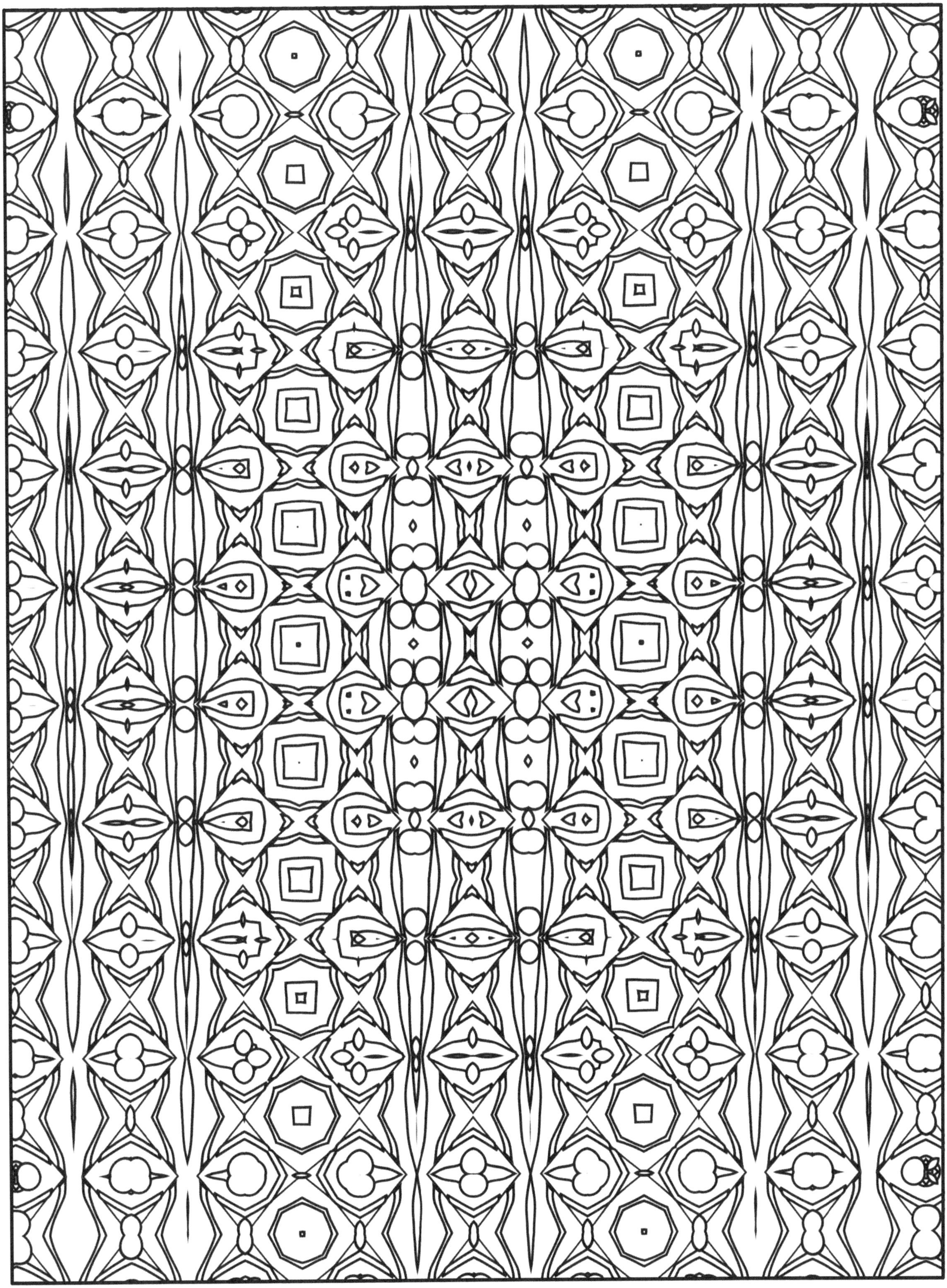

www.ingramcontent.com/pod-product-compliance
Lightning Source LLC
Chambersburg PA
CBHW080848220526
45467CB00008B/2425
* 9 7 9 8 7 0 5 4 6 9 4 5 1 *